Pocket Rough Guide

Copenhagen

This second edition updated by

JANE GRAHAM

Contents

INTRODUCTION TO

Copenhagen

Once a low-key underrated city, for the past decade, the Danish capital has been showered with superlatives, with polls claiming it to have the best quality of life and rating its citizens the happiest people on the planet. If that wasn't enough, accolades for its cuisine, metro, cycling and design have followed, and Danish TV dramas continue to bring its Nordic style, gritty architecture and photo-genic inhabitants into millions of living rooms. Despite its new-found glory, Copenhagen remains a relaxed, homely place where visitors quickly feel at ease; and while all this cool contentment doesn't come cheap (for tourists and locals alike) the "great Dane" has quite definitely arrived as one of Europe's outstanding destinations.

AMAGERTORV

Best places to explore on two wheels

Cycling is a way of life in Copenhagen – nearly everyone gets to school and work on two wheels. Pick up a snazzy bike for rent at Københavns Cykelbørs in Indre By, then pedal around Christianshavn's quiet canals, up to Kastellet to see the Little Mermaid or out to Frederiksberg's lush parks. Alternatively, hop on a train (bike in tow) up the coast, then pedal out to see the world-class art of the Louisiana Museum or around Kronborg Castle, one of the most handsome fortresses in the land.

Part of Copenhagen's appeal is its hybrid nature, a unique blend of mainland Europe and Scandinavia. The city looks as much to London, Berlin and Amsterdam as it does to Stockholm or Oslo, perhaps a legacy of its swashbuckling seafaring and trading history. Its gregarious English-speaking inhabitants can also seem positively welcoming compared with the icy reserve of their northerly neighbours.

If the city lacks anything you could say it's a true "blockbuster" attraction. Aside from the Little Mermaid and arguably the Tivoli Gardens, Copenhagen doesn't do the "queue round the block" tourism, while its most illustrious former inhabitants (Hans Christian Andersen aside) don't quite make the global pilgrimage hit list. Instead you'll discover a marvellously eclectic range of

museums, galleries, designer shops and royal heritage buildings, all easily digestible and perfect for short-break perusing. For an idea of where to begin turn to our itineraries and "best of" sections.

Whether you're on foot, cycling (see box above) or jumping on the user-friendly transport system you'll also find Copenhagen eminently navigable. You can quickly flit between neighbourhoods, from the cobbled avenues of Frederiksstaden and grand Slotsholmen island to the winding medieval streets of the Latin Quarter and the gritty boho chic of Nørrebro. Green space and charming canals are never far away, whether in the landscaped Kongens Have, or postcard-cute Nyhavn. For those schooled in Dansk design and architecture a visit to Christianshavn will reveal the city's more adventurous

NYHAVN

When to visit

Easily Copenhagen's best season is summer, when both locals and visitors stay out nursing their drinks until the wee hours and cultural events such as the ten-day-long Copenhagen Jazz Festival bring live music, dance and art to the streets. Autumn and spring are similarly alluring – especially for cycling – since the afternoons remain warm but the majority of tourists have departed. Still, don't write off winter, a perfectly charming time for drinking *gløgg* (Scandinavian mulled wine) in cosy bars and enjoying the beloved Danish tradition of *hygge* (cosiness). The festive markets of Tivoli and Nyhavn and the Christmas lights make the city an excellent destination for a festive break.

side: big open skies and sleek glass and chrome modernism. Come nightfall and another Copenhagen emerges – Michelin-star chefs shout out orders, cocktails are shaken and craft beers cracked open (see opposite for the best neighbourhoods to try).

Given Denmark itself is small, the capital is nearby some other cracking destinations. Half an hour west is medieval Roskilde, home to a superb museum of Viking ships, one of Europe's biggest music festivals, and a brand-new museum of rock music opened at the end of 2015. North of the capital, meanwhile, stands the outstanding modern art museum of Louisiana, the picture-perfect Renaissance castle of Kronborg and – across the iconic Øresund Bridge – the cool, diminutive Swedish city of Malmö, once part of Denmark's regal orbit.

COPENHAGEN AT A GLANCE

>> EATING

At the time of writing the Danish capital boasted a record eighteen Michelin stars – more than anywhere else in Scandinavia (see box, p.72). While advance booking at the better-known dining spots is recommended, Copenhagen isn't all haute cuisine: you can also find great local and international spots such as Christianshavn's *Bådudlejning, Café* and *Ølhalle* and *Pintxos* which will suit slightly slimmer purses. Furthermore, restaurants all over the city often offer affordable lunchtime options, and you can always visit Nørrebro's Torvehallerne market for everything from organic wines to freshly baked goods – especially on Sundays, when many city restaurants close their doors anyway.

>> DRINKING

Danes, apparently, drink more coffee than anywhere else in the world, and downtown Copenhagen is paradise for caffeine addicts – *Café Norden* and *Café Europe* are two of Indre By's most popular. Many daytime cafés often morph into cosy and candlelit bars come eveningtime, and nearly anywhere in Copenhagen you can find music lilting from inside a chilled bar until very late – perfect for enjoying a relaxing pint of Carlsberg or one of Denmark's many excellent microbrews (don't miss Ølfabrikken's traditional stouts). Most recently, the city has acquired some great wine

bars, most notably in Vesterbro and Nørrebro.

>> NIGHTLIFE

If you're in the market for late nights out, the trendy meatpacking district of Kødbyen should be your first – or, rather, last – stop. This recently gentrified neighbourhood of lofts and warehouses has become one of Europe's hottest places to party with DJs, live bands and plenty of dancing. For something more mellow, try Sankt Hans Torv and the surrounding streets in Nørrebro, probably the best place in the city for a romantic late-night drink. Don't miss a shot of ice-cold caraway schnapps – a Danish speciality.

>> SHOPPING

To get your retail kicks, the central cobbled pedestrian Strøget offers large department stores, including Illums Bolighus, a favourite with the Danish queen, plus iconic local brands Royal Copenhagen and Georg Jensen. The nearby streets of Købmagergade and Kompagnistræde have small, independent holes-in-the-wall selling modern design objets and housewares, while the student-filled Latin Quarter is the place to head for secondhand fashion. South, Værnedamsvej in Vesterbro is great for local designers, while northerly Nørrebro (especially Elmegade and Blågårdsgade) offers chic shops with designers on hand to tailor the clothing on the racks to fit you perfectly.

OUR RECOMMENDATIONS FOR WHERE TO EAT, DRINK AND SHOP ARE LISTED AT THE END OF EACH CHAPTER.

Day One in Copenhagen

1 Latin Quarter, Inner City > p.39.
Begin the day strolling about this maze
of lively medieval streets and squares
around Copenhagen University, perfect
for losing yourself in history.

2 Rådhus > p.36. Climb to the
tower of this grandiose, National
Romantic city hall, whose fascinating
astronomical clock is a destination
in itself.

Lunch > *Aamanns* (see
p.74). This rustic-urban
eatery does modern takes on the
traditional Danish smørrebrød.

3 Canal Tour > p.131. Join one of
the multilingual hourly tours along
Copenhagen's centuries-old canals,
which offer fascinating insight into
important events and sights tied to
Denmark's tumultuous history.

4 Rosenborg Slot > p.68. Explore
your inner royal at this fairy-tale,
red-brick Renaissance castle, whose
cellar holds the Danish crown jewels
and Frederik III's coronation throne,
made of gold and narwhal tusk.

5 Nyboder > p.73. Make your way
out to the multicoloured terraced
houses in this relaxed part of town,
built in the seventeenth century to
house the Danish navy.

Dinner > *Toldboden* (see
p.67). This spacious, casual
restaurant is set opposite the royal
yacht's mooring and is unbeatable for
people-watching.

6 The Little Mermaid > p.63. Stroll
out to Kastellet to catch a glimpse of
Copenhagen's mascot and the heroine
of Hans Christian Andersen's fairy tale.

Day Two in Copenhagen

1 Ny Carlsberg Glyptotek > p.34. Start off in this brilliant museum, which holds a vast classical and modern European art collection displayed in opulent rooms.

2 Orlogsmuseet > p.80. Hundreds of Danish military ships from the seventeenth century onwards are on display at the Danish Naval Museum, including one for children to clamber on.

3 Christiania > p.80. Amble along the pretty Christianshavns Kanal, designed by an Amsterdam-born architect, before exploring this renowned hippie "free city" commune.

Lunch > *Cofoco* (see p.92). Enjoy a variety of scrumptious "Nordic tapas" from a long and seasonally changing menu at this popular spot.

4 Frederiksberg Have > p.90. Pedal out towards Værnedamsvej for a spot of fashionista window shopping, then put down on the open expanses of grass at the city's most wild parklands.

5 Musikmuseet > p.88. Giraffe pianos are just some of the unusual instruments on display at the Music Museum, which reopened in DR's former Radio House in 2014.

6 Helsingør > p.109. Ride the train up the coast to watch the sun set against Kronborg, a fairy-tale fortress and the inspiration for Elsinore Castle in Shakespeare's *Hamlet*.

Dinner > *Brasserie Nimb* (see p.37). Great traditional French food with a regularly changing menu in an Oriental-style palace, located on the edge of the Tivoli Gardens.

Kids' Copenhagen

Families will find plenty to keep the kids happy from amusement parks to swimming pools, science museums to playgrounds.

1 Tivoli > p.32. This magical fairground has roller coasters, pantomime theatres and endless helpings of family fun.

2 Havneparken > p.82. Combine shopping with swimming at Fisketorvet's Copencabana, popular with children thanks to its two outdoor pools and diving boards built right into the harbour.

3 Rundetårn > p.39. This 42m-high stone church tower has an observatory at the top offering great vistas across to the city's numerous spires.

Lunch > Café Hovedtelegrafen (see p.46). Kids' tapas plate and glorious views from the rooftop restaurant of the Post & Tele Museum.

4 Tøjhusmuseet > p.56. Denmark's national arsenal museum is filled with swords, firearms, cannons and umpteen warfare accoutrements.

5 Ridebane > p.54. Visit the Royal Stables, whose regal, marble-clad stables are home to golden carriages and beautiful horses.

6 Experimentarium > p.99. This huge science lab lets kids learn about the human body, physics and the natural world, all with hands-on high-energy exhibits.

Dinner > Madklubben (see p.66 & p.93). This much-loved Danish chain offers delicious meals at surprisingly affordable prices.

Budget Copenhagen

Though Copenhagen is Europe's third most expensive capital, you can save cash by using a discount card, riding free city bikes, taking harbour bus-boats and visiting many of the city's free-entry museums.

1 National Museum > p.36. Home to Denmark's finest ethnographic artefacts, including an extensive collection of Viking weapons and coins.

2 Amalienborg > p.60. A few metres from the harbourfront, soldiers participate in the Changing of the Guard here at noon every day.

Lunch > Pick up some bread, cheese and drinks, then picnic on the grass of Kongens Have (see p.69), the city's most popular green space.

3 Marmorkirken > p.61. This marble church was built in 1894 in the image of St Peter's in Rome; join the 1pm tour to ascend the 260 steps to the dome's apogee for some grand city views.

4 Slotsholmen > p.52. Descend a narrow stairwell to explore the ruins of two excavated underground castles.

5 Assistens Kirkegaard > p.96. Cross the western lakes to take in the final resting place of Danish luminaries such as Hans Christian Andersen and Niels Bohr.

6 Galerie Asbæk > p.64. This much-loved gallery represents some of Denmark's best-known painters and photographers and is great for a spot of window shopping.

Dinner > *Vespa* (see p.67). This simple, down-at-heel Italian restaurant's four-course set menus are outstanding value for money.

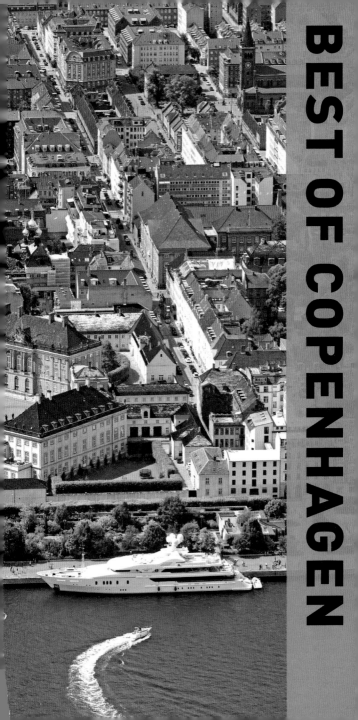

BEST OF COPENHAGEN

Architecture

1 The Black Diamond This stunning piece of waterfront modernism is both a concert hall and a super spot for people-watching. > **p.57**

2 Marmorkirken Taking 145 years to complete, this grandiose marble church has a specatular bell tower, reached by climbing 260 tortuous steps. > **p.61**

3 Skuespilhuset The sleek and modern Royal Danish playhouse is a wonderful spot for lunch. > **p.61**

4 Rundetårn Christian IV's 40m tower, accessed by a unique spiral walkway, provides one of the best vantage points over the city. > **p.39**

5 Carlsberg Byen The historic Carslberg quarter is full of quirky architecural features, including the wonderful Elephant Gate. > **p.89**

Eating

1 Laundromat Wonderful little café that doubles as a launderette. Brilliant burgers and fries, which you can linger over while playing backgammon. > **p.102**

2 Madklubben Not a mad choice at all – delicious, affordable food from this popular chain (branches in central Copenhagen and Vesterbro). **> p.66 & 93**

3 Copenhagen Street Food Over thirty food stands and healthy fast-food trucks on Papirøen in Holmen, most of it organic and locally sourced. **> p.84**

4 Aamanns Stylish restaurant that has reinvented the Danish smørrebrød (open sandwich), with fresh, innovative ingredients. **> p.74**

5 La Glace You haven't tried a true Danish pastry until you've visited this Copenhagen icon, open since 1870. Also does legendary ice cream. **> p.47**

Art

1 Ny Carlsberg Glyptotek From Classical Roman sculptures to French impressionists, some of Europe's most enviable art resides at this glass-domed, palm-filled museum. > **p.34**

2 Hirschsprungske Samling A wonderfully intimate gallery showcasing Danish masterpieces from the collection of Heinrich Hirschsprung. > **p.71**

4 Christiania The "free city" showcases evocative street art painted on its ramparts, walls and shacks – well worth exploring. > **p.80**

3 Statens Museum for Kunst Denmark's national gallery provides everything from Italian religious art to Picasso and Matisse. > **p.70**

5 Louisiana Amble away a day in the twisting corridors of this unique museum, known for its Giacomettis, Rodchenkos and Warhols. > **p.108**

Shopping

1 Strøget Big department stores rub shoulders with small independent boutiques along the world's longest pedestrianized street. **> p.38**

2 Torvehallerne An atmospheric covered food market purveying upscale Danish delicacies and prime produce. > **p.73**

3 Royal Copenhagen Head to the porcelain giant's flagship store for stylish gifts and kitchenware. > **p.45**

4 Ecouture by Lund Unique and environmentally conscious fashion created by local costume designer Johanne Helger Lund. > **p.43**

5 Paustian High-end designer furniture and more affordable accessories sold in a beautifully designed building. > **p.100**

Waterfront

1 Havneparken Brace yourself for a dip in the Harbour Park pool, a favourite hangout in summer (and open on New Year's Day should you fancy it). > **p.82**

2 Nyhavn This quaint much-photographed harbour is located just alongside a strip of popular bars and restaurants. > **p.58**

3 Christianshavns Kanal Stroll (or kayak) about one of Copenhagen's quietest, most handsome canals, right in the heart of the city. > **p.78**

4 Amager Strandpark Just south of the city, this clean sandy beach has views of the Øresund bridge. > **p.110**

5 Halvandet Urban beach bar that's a favourite with the beautiful people, who come for the laidback beats and cool, Ibiza-esque vibe. > **p.85**

Drinking

1 **Alfresco bars** Summer or winter, Danes have perfected the art of outdoor drinking —try Nyhavn, Vesterbro and Nørrebro **> p.67, p.94 & p.104**

2 Kødbyen Copenhagen's meatpacking district is the hippest area for a night out. **> p.88**

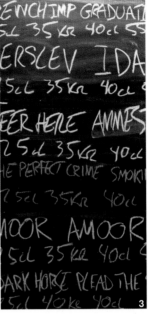

3 Ølbaren Serving literally hundreds of different European beers, this Nørrebro institution is a must for beer geeks. **> p.105**

4 Oak Room Swinging little joint serving fabulous cocktails including the Slutty Mary, a tequila-infused Bloody Mary with lime, coriander and chilli. **> p.105**

5 Mikkeller An elegant, modernist pub appealing both to craft ale hipsters and design fans thanks to its beautifully constructed interior. **> p.95**

Museums

1 National Museum World-class collection of historical artefacts, from bog people and fifteenth-century BC sculptures to Viking weapons. > **p.36**

2 Thorvaldsens Museum Copenhagen-born Bertel Thorvaldsen was one of Europe's finest Neoclassical sculptors. Here you'll find his greatest works including *Jason with the Golden Fleece*. > **p.55**

3 Experimentarium This massive science centre will keep the kids entertained for hours. > **p.99**

4 Designmuseum Denmark Trace the evolution of Danish design from Renaissance textiles to Arne Jacobsen chairs – Ikea it ain't. > **p.62**

5 Blue Planet Opened in March 2013, this jaw-dropping modern aquarium holds some 20,000 animals across 450 species. > **p.110**

Royalty

1 Guards at Amalienborg Kids love the royal palace's poker-faced guards, who ceremoniously change their position every day at noon. **> p.60**

2 Frederiksborg Fairy-tale renaissance castle spread out across several small islands, featuring a lake, gardens, Gothic towers and spires. **> p.109**

3 Crown jewels Swords, sceptres and gilded crowns, kept safe in the basement at Rosenborg Slot **> p.68**

4 Reception Rooms Tapestries Bjørn Nørgaard's technicolour modern tapestries are hung high in the Great Hall, showcasing the history of Denmark. **> p.52**

5 Royal Stables Coaches, carriages and around twenty particularly well-groomed steeds. **> p.54**

PLACES

Tivoli and Rådhuspladsen

Tivoli, Denmark's most-visited attraction, may appear at first glance every bit as tacky as any other amusement park around the world, but it has much more to offer than just its thrilling set of rides. After taking in the 83,000-square-metre gardens, with their gorgeous flower displays and fountains, romantic boating lake, exotic-looking buildings (from Chinese pagodas to Moorish palaces) and – at night – spectacular illuminations, even the most cynical visitor will have to succumb and agree that it's a magical (albeit expensive) place. A few paces away is the buzzing Rådhuspladsen square, towered over by the grand red-brick nineteenth-century city hall, whose innards hold a fascinating astronomical clock. As well as demarcating the city's geographical heart, the square is the perfect place for a mustard-topped *pølse*.

TIVOLI

Vesterbrogade 3 ☎ 33 15 10 01, ⓦ tivoli.dk. April 1 to mid-Sept, three weeks in Oct & mid-Nov to Jan 3 Mon–Thurs & Sun 11am–11pm, Fri & Sat 11am–midnight. Adults and children aged 8 and over 99kr; under-8s free. Rides 25–75kr, multi-ride pass 209kr.
MAP OPPOSITE, POCKET MAP A13

Opened in 1843, **Tivoli** was the creation of architect George Carstensen, who had been commissioned by Christian VIII to build a pleasure garden for the masses outside the western gate into the city. It was an immediate success, and – expanded and modernized over the years – was a major influence on Walt Disney for his theme parks a century later. That the gardens continue even today to occupy such a patch of prime real estate, sandwiched

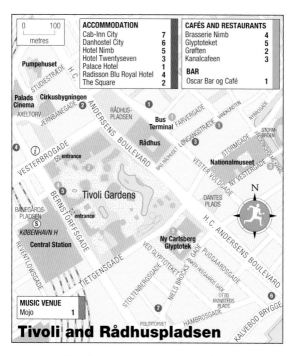

Tivoli and Rådhuspladsen

between the Hovedbanegården and the Rådhus, is testimony to Tivoli's central place within the city's affections.

Tivoli's principal draw, of course – to children at least – is its twenty-five-odd **rides**, which include one of the world's oldest still-functioning wooden roller coasters. Still more hair-raising are the Star Flyer, which lifts up and twirls thrill-seekers around some 80m above ground, and Aquila, which thrusts its victims around at the nauseating force of 4G. Music, theatre and panto (mostly free once you're in) are a key part of Tivoli's appeal, with over five stages and several bandstands. Pantomime – in the classic Italian *commedia dell'arte* tradition – is put on throughout the year in the extraordinary Chinese-style

Pantomime Theatre, and every Friday evening in season at 10pm there's a hugely popular gig (Ⓦfredagsrock.dk) at the open-air **Plænen** stage, featuring mainly Scandinavian acts. The gardens can get crowded but the setting is magical and the atmosphere buzzing – and Tivoli's undulating layout means that you can always find a peaceful and picturesque nook from which to relax and drink in the scene.

Formerly only open during summertime, in recent years Tivoli has extended its season to include three weeks leading up to **Halloween**, when the gardens are bestrewn with smiley pumpkins and clingy cobwebs, and a six-week **Christmas market**, when the best of Danish Yuletide traditions are on show.

What lies beneath: digging up the town

With a brand-new orbital metro line due to open in 2019, large parts of the old city are currently under excavation, the most extensive building work since Christian IV (aka the builder king) erected most of Copenhagen's defensive works, castles and churches in the sixteenth century. **Archeologists** from the Københavns Museum (currently closed due to relocation) are having a field day (literally) unlocking the city's underground secrets before the diggers are let loose, and some aspects of its history are now under revision. New data has emerged indicating, for example, that a major settlement existed here before Bishop Absalon founded Copenhagen in the twelfth century and that the settlers at the time were much taller than previously thought. **The WALL**, an interactive mobile 12-metre screen, follows the excavators around, providing above-ground news on the latest finds and discoveries underneath. For information on where to find it, consult ⓦ m.dk and ⓦ copenhagen.dk.

CENTRAL STATION

MAP P.33, POCKET MAP A14

Designed by station builder extraordinaire Heinrich Wenck as a *Gesamtkunstwerk* (total work of art), the hulking yet elegant **Hovedbanegården** (Central Station) is one of the country's most noteworthy National Romantic buildings. Dating from 1911, it's built predominantly in red brick, slate and granite, as dictated by the style, with abundant decorative detail – all of which Wenck was responsible for. Note in particular the large wood-beamed (rather than cast-iron) arches supporting the roof structure above the central hall and platforms, and the magnificent chandeliers.

The station is home to the studio of a national television channel, TV2. Journalists from the daily *Go'morgen Danmark* ("Good Morning Denmark") breakfast show often canvass opinions on the issues of the day from passing travellers, so don't be surprised if you're suddenly stopped for a quick interview.

NY CARLSBERG GLYPTOTEK

Dantes Plads 7 ☎ 33 41 81 41, ⓦ glyptoteket .dk. Tues, Wed & Fri–Sun 11am–6pm, Thurs 11am–10pm; 95kr, free on Tues. Free guided tours in English mid-June to mid-Sept noon & 1pm (rest of the year in Danish only). MAP P.33, POCKET MAP B14

Impossible to miss with its opulent red-brick Venetian Renaissance facade, the exquisite **Ny Carlsberg Glyptotek** was established by brewing magnate Carl Jacobsen (1842–1914) to

NY CARLSBERG GLYPTOTEK

provide a public home for his vast private art collection. The building and collection have since been extended and expanded several times, the gallery's richly decorated rooms providing as captivating a spectacle as the remarkable haul of ancient and modern works on display.

The main entrance takes you into the museum's original building (1897), designed by Danish architect **Vilhelm Dahlerup**. Housed within its two floors of extravagantly colourful friezes, marble pillars and mosaic floors are sculptures and paintings from the **Danish Golden Age**, including Bertel Thorvaldsen's evocative *The Three Graces* relief, and a fine collection of **French sculpture**, with particular emphasis on Rodin – the largest collection of his work outside France. The undoubted highlight of the Dahlerup section, however, is the tranquil, glass-domed **Winter Garden** around which it centres, filled with palm trees, statues and a fountain. The museum café here serves arguably Scandinavia's best cake (see p.37).

On the opposite side of the Winter Garden, the large marble-pillared Central Hall of the elaborate **Kampmann**

NY CARLSBERG GLYPTOTEK

extension (1905) leads to an extensive **Ancient Mediterranean** collection, which starts around 6000 BC and traces the development of the Greek, Etruscan and Roman empires. From the Central Hall a set of stairs leads up to a newer wing designed by Henning Larsen (of the Opera House; see p.82), a courtyard infill housing a fantastic collection of **French post-impressionist** paintings including noteworthy pieces by Degas, Manet and Gauguin.

Axeltorv Square: circus friezes and multicoloured facades

Vesterport, once the western gate into the city, has some notable architectural landmarks. Cirkusbygningen ("the Circus Building") was built in the 1880s; note the elaborate horse-racing frieze that still encircles the building. Now a venue for dinner shows, in its heyday the adjoining stables stretched as far as Studiestræde and housed circus horses, giraffes and elephants. On the other side of Axeltorv, 17-screen Palads cinema opened in 1912, its brightly coloured facade added in 1989 by Danish abstract artist Poul Gerners. The building site opposite is the ghost of the Scala entertainment complex, which despite its popularity in the 1990s was torn down in 2012; five grandly designed, landmark office towers are envisioned in its place.

THE RÅDHUS

Rådhuspladsen ☎ 33 66 33 66. Mon–Fri 9am–4pm, Sat 1am–1pm. Access to Jens Olsen's World Clock 10kr. Tower Mon–Fri 11am & 2pm, Sat noon; 30kr; Tours in English Mon–Fri 1pm, Sat 10am, 50kr. MAP P.33, POCKET MAP B13

Dominating Rådhuspladsen, the city's bustling cobbled main square (much of it currently cordoned off by metro building works), is the grand **Rådhus** (City Hall) from 1905, a great example of the National Romantic style with beautiful and intricate decorative detail throughout. Just past the entrance, the stately main hall has walls of layered polished red brick and limestone (a reference to the national flag) and an impressive arched gallery, beneath which a limestone strip is inscribed with key moments in Copenhagen's history. As a working public building the City Hall is open to visitors, though the informative **tours** are the best way to capture its full detail. Tours include access to the 105m **tower**, which gives stunning views of the city, and **Jens Olsen's world clock** – an extraordinary astronomical timepiece from 1955 with hundreds of ticking dials tracking the planetary movement with astounding accuracy.

NATIONALMUSEET

Ny Vestergade 10 ☎ 33 13 44 11. ⓦ natmus.dk. Tues–Sun 10am–5pm. Free. MAP P.33, POCKET MAP C13

Housed in an eighteenth-century Rococo palace, formerly the Danish Crown Prince's residence, the immense **National Museum**'s vast collection, which stretches from prehistory to the present day via the Viking period and Middle Ages, could easily take days to

NATIONALMUSEET

go through. If you're short of time, head straight for the second floor and the captivating **Inuit** part of the vast **Ethnographic** collection, the most extensive of its kind in the world. There's a wealth of detail on their hunting techniques and exhibits include dog sledges and some amazing hand-carved kayaks. It also provides a succinct account of the events leading to Denmark's colonization of Greenland. Standout among the exhibits in the **Danish prehistory** section are the magical gold-plated Trundholm Sun Chariot, dating from around 1400 BC, which has featured on many a Danish stamp since its discovery in 1902, and – above all – the bog-preserved **Egtved Girl** (1370 BC), who still has her clothes, hair and jewellery intact. Finally, a detour to the **Viking exhibition** will categorically banish the perception that all Vikings did was rape and pillage. Room 23 gives an insight into the remarkable distances they travelled – as far as present-day Iran and Afghanistan – on their trade and diplomatic missions to gather silver, the main currency of the era.

Cafés and restaurants

BRASSERIE NIMB

Bernstorffsgade 5 ☎ 88 70 00 10, ⓦ nimb.dk.
MAP P.33, POCKET MAP A13

One of four restaurants within the lavish *Nimb Hotel*, Tivoli's romantic fairy-tale *Arabian Nights*-style palace (though also accessible from outside the gardens), the ground-floor *Brasserie* is a temple to traditional French cuisine. Open throughout the year.

GLYPTOTEKET

Dantes Plads 7 ☎ 33 41 81 28,
ⓦ glyptoteket.dk. Tues–Sun 11am–6pm.
MAP P.33, POCKET MAP B14

Even if the Ny Carlsberg Glyptotek's art and sculpture don't grab you, it's worth visiting the café, occupying a beautiful position in the glass-domed Winter Garden, for exquisite smørrebrød (from 110kr) and cake (from 45kr).

GRØFTEN

Tivoli ☎ 33 75 06 75, ⓦ groeften.dk. See Tivoli for opening hrs. MAP P.33, POCKET MAP A13

Historic restaurant with seating outdoors on a large open terrace, popular with celebs of a certain vintage. The overloaded prawn sandwich (125kr) and the all-you-can-eat *skipperlabskovs* (Danish goulash; 165kr) are legendary, as is the smørrebrød (from 75kr).

KANALCAFEEN

Frederiksholms Kanal 18 ☎ 33 11 57 70,
ⓦ kanalcafeen.dk. Mon–Fri 11.30am–5pm,
Sat 11.30am–3pm. MAP P.33, POCKET MAP C13

Founded in 1852, this cosy, historic lunchtime restaurant opposite Christiansborg serves outstanding, good-value smørrebrød (from 59kr for marinated herring). Inside, the decor is all heavy tablecloths and period oil paintings, while outside there's canalside seating in summer.

Bar

OSCAR BAR OG CAFÉ

Rådhuspladsen 77 ☎ 33 12 09 99,
ⓦ oscarbarcafe.dk. Sun–Thurs 11am–11pm,
Fri & Sat 11am–2am. MAP P.33, POCKET MAP B13

Set just next to the Rådhus, this very popular gay bar is lively and well lit, and has DJs pumping tunes out until late on weekends. Happy hour (5–9pm) has 33kr Carlsbergs, and there are good sandwiches and burgers (from 79kr) too.

Music venue

MOJO

Løngangstræde 21C ☎ 33 11 64 53, ⓦ mojo
.dk. Daily 8pm–5am. MAP P.33, POCKET MAP C13

This authentic, smoky bar with sticky beer-stained tables is a must for blues aficionados. The live gigs (most nights from 9.30pm) are usually free, though chargeable (up to 150kr) when bigger names are playing.

GRØFTEN

Strøget and the Inner City

Indre By ("inner city") is Copenhagen's heart and hub, its compact warren of narrow streets and cobbled squares home to the capital's principal shopping district and countless bars and restaurants. For centuries Indre By was Copenhagen, springing into life with the arrival of Bishop Absalon in 1167, and fortified with stone walls until the nineteenth century. Historic buildings rub shoulders with modern but the area, bisected by the bustling pedestrianized thoroughfare of Strøget, is at its most atmospheric around the Latin Quarter, original home to the university, and pretty, colourful Gråbrødre Torv.

STRØGET

MAP PP.40–41, POCKET MAP B12–D11

The principal artery of the city's main shopping district, **Strøget** is a series of five interconnecting pedestrian streets, over 1km in length, which runs from Rådhuspladsen to Kongens Nytorv (see p.42). One of the world's first pedestrian strips when it was created in 1962, it's abuzz with life 24/7 from the constant flow of shoppers during the day and revellers at night. Street entertainers and fruit and snack sellers also ply their trade – the weeks before Christmas are especially lively, with carol singers, shoppers galore and delicious treats – such as *æbleskiver* (sweet, deep-fried apple dumplings) and *gløgg* (mulled wine) on sale.

The Rådhuspladsen end of Strøget, beginning with **Frederiksberggade**, is fairly tacky but the strip gradually goes more upmarket, running past some of the city's oldest buildings and squares. On **Gammeltorv** (Old Square), look out for the **Caritas Fountain**, which predates the (much more famous) Manneken Pis in Brussels, and features a woman spraying water from her breasts as a small boy pees into the basin.

AMAGERTORV

From here, Strøget continues past Amagertorv (see p.41), culminating in a line of exclusive designer stores as it reaches Østergade and Kongens Nytorv (see p.42).

RUNDETÅRN

Købmagergade 52A ☎ 33 73 03 73, ⓦ rundetaarn.dk. Tower: daily mid-May to Sept 10am–8pm; Oct to mid-May 10am–6pm. Observatory: mid-Oct to mid-March Tues & Wed 7–9pm. 25kr MAP PP.40–41, POCKET MAP C11

Built by Christian IV in the mid-seventeenth century, the 42m-high **Rundetårn** (Round Tower) originally formed part of a larger complex, functioning both as church tower and **observatory**. The observatory, at the top of the tower, is still operational – the oldest of its kind still in use in Europe – and can be visited in wintertime, while the ascent, along a wide, cobbled walkway, is straightforward even for vertigo sufferers. As you make your way up, you can catch your breath at the **modern art gallery** in the former university library hall, and at the various other quirky exhibits en route, including Christian IV's toilet. The view from the top, across the city's many towers and spires, is fabulous.

RUNDETÅRN

THE LATIN QUARTER

Frue Plads. MAP PP.40–41, POCKET MAP B11

In one of the city's most historic areas, the buildings of the so-called **Latin Quarter** around Fiolstræde date back to the foundation of Scandinavia's earliest university in 1475. Hailing from 1836, the grand neo-Gothic **university** building across Frue Plads from Vor Frue Kirke serves a primarily administrative purpose today – most of the university departments have relocated outside the city centre. On one side a row of busts of the university's rationalist scholars – including Nobel prize-winning Niels Bohr – faces off against busts of religious men lining the cathedral wall opposite.

HELLIGÅNDSKIRKEN

Amagertorv. Mon–Fri noon–4pm (plus services on Sun). MAP PP.40–41, POCKET MAP C12

One of the city's oldest churches, dating back to the thirteenth century, the **Helligåndskirken** (Church of the Holy Ghost) was originally part of a Catholic monastery. Following the Reformation it became a Lutheran church, and although repeatedly destroyed (by fire and bombardment), an evocative section of the monastery, the **Helligåndshuset**, survives in the church's west wing (to the left of the entrance) as the city's largest and most intact medieval building. It's not hard to imagine its past incarnation as a medieval hospital, beds crammed in between the slender granite columns that hold up the heavy vaulted ceiling. Today it houses regular flea markets, concerts and exhibitions.

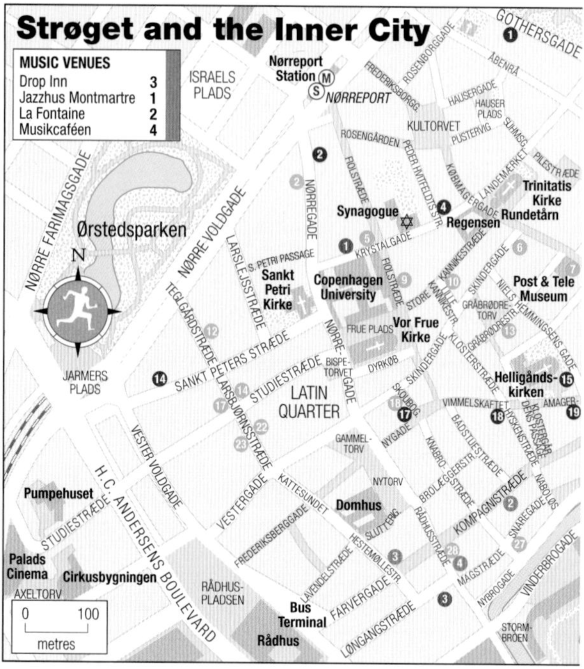

Strøget and the Inner City

MUSIC VENUES	
Drop Inn	3
Jazzhus Montmartre	1
La Fontaine	2
Musikcaféen	4

Map labels: GOTHERSGADE, ABENRÅ, Nørreport Station, FREDERIKSBORGGADE, ROSENBORGGADE, HAUSER PLADS, ISRAELS PLADS, NØRREPORT, KULTORVET, PUSTERVIG, ROSENGÅRDEN, PEDER HVITFELDTS., KØBMAGERGADE, LANDEMÆRKET, PILESTRÆDE, Trinitatis Kirke, Rundetårn, NØRRE FARIMAGSGADE, Ørstedsparken, NØRREGADE, Synagogue, Regensen, KRYSTALGADE, SUHMSGADE, KANNIKESTRÆDE, Post & Tele Museum, NØRRE VOLDGADE, LARSLEJSTRÆDE, S. PETRI PASSAGE, Sankt Petri Kirke, Copenhagen University, FIOLSTRÆDE, STORE KANNIKE, Vor Frue Kirke, SKINDERGADE, GRÅBRØDRE TORV, KLOSTERGADE, VALKENDORFSGADE, TEGLGÅRDSTRÆDE, FRUE PLADS, NØRRE, BISPE-TORVET, DYRKØB, KLOSTERSTR., Helligånds-kirken, JARMERS PLADS, SANKT PETERS STRÆDE, STUDIESTRÆDE, LARSBJØRNSSTRÆDE, LATIN QUARTER, VIMMELSKAFTET, BADSTUESTRÆDE, AMAGERTORV, VESTERGADE, GAMMEL-TORV, NYGADE, KNABRO, H. C. ANDERSENS BOULEVARD, KATTESUNDET, NYTORV, BROLÆGGERSTRÆDE, KOMPAGNISTRÆDE, Pumpehuset, STUDIESTRÆDE, VESTERGADE, Domhus, FREDERIKSBERGGADE, RÅDHUSSTR., MAGSTRÆDE, NYBROGADE, Palads Cinema, Cirkusbygningen, RÅDHUS-PLADSEN, AXELTORV, Bus Terminal, LAVENDELSTRÆDE, FARVERGADE, LØNGANGSTRÆDE, VINDERBROGADE, STORM-BROEN, Rådhus

```
0        100
    metres
```

VOR FRUE KIRKE

Frue Plads ☎ 33 15 10 78,
ⓦ koebenhavnsdomkirke.dk. Daily 8am–5pm,
except during services. MAP ABOVE, POCKET MAP B11

The plain, rather sombre-looking **Vor Frue Kirke** (Church of Our Lady) dates from 1829 and has functioned as Copenhagen's cathedral since 1923, though there's been a church on this site since the eleventh century. It's not until you're through the heavy Doric-pillared portal into the whitewashed Neoclassical interior that its more elegant features are revealed. A simple carved frieze above the altar accentuates a magnificent statue of Christ by Bertel Thorvaldsen (see p.55); the statue's hand positioning gave Thorvaldsen much grief before he finally decided on the open downward-facing position appreciated by both Catholics and Protestants alike. In 2004, the cathedral briefly hit the international spotlight as the

VOR FRUE KIRKE

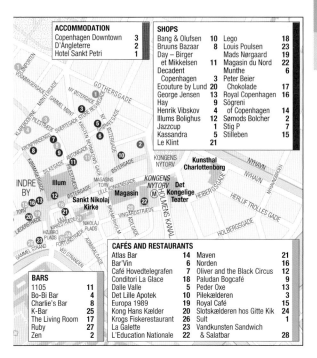

venue for the wedding of Crown Prince Frederik and his Tasmanian wife Mary.

AMAGERTORV AND HØJBRO PLADS

MAP ABOVE, POCKET MAP C12–D12

If Strøget has a focal point, it's the L-shaped interconnecting squares of **Amagertorv** and **Højbro Plads**. On the direct route between the once royal residence of Christiansborg and Vor Frue Kirke these two squares have borne witness to numerous coronation parties, royal weddings and (prior to the Reformation) religious processions. They're especially bustling in summertime when the cafés set up outside and snack vendors and bicycle-rickshaw operators ply their trade. Tourists seem perpetu-

ally drawn to pose by the two artworks by sculptor Vilhem Bissen: an equestrian statue of Bishop Absalon and the *Storkespringvandet* (Stork Fountain), while a more recent addition is the beautiful mosaic paving by Bjørn Nørgaard (see p.53).

KØBMAGERGADE AND AROUND

MAP ABOVE, POCKET MAP D11

On the corner of Strøget and the busy pedestrianized side street of **Købmagergade**, the Illum department store is one of the city's top places to shop, full of labels including Acne and Paul Smith. Running off Købmagergade to the east is a super-trendy knot of lanes – most notably **Pilestræde** – littered with exclusive designer shops.

POST & TELE MUSEUM

Købmagergade 37 ☎ 33 41 09 00,
ⓦ ptt-museum.dk. Daily 10am–4pm. Free.
MAP PP.40–41, POCKET MAP C11

The **Post & Tele Museum** is devoted to the history of communication, from the establishment of the country's first post office in 1624 (another Scandinavian first) up to now, taking in floors and floors of old stagecoaches, early computers and probably the best stamp collection in the world en route. Most fascinating is the – by its nature – constantly changing exhibition on the future of communications, though best of all is the wonderful rooftop café (see p.46) that offers fine views of downtown Copenhagen.

KONGENS NYTORV

MAP PP.40–41, POCKET MAP E11

The city's grandest square, **Kongens Nytorv** was for years the main entrance to the royal part of the city. It is currently largely hidden behind a metro construction site, and unlikely to be accessible before 2017. The "King's New Square" was laid out in 1670 by Christian V as part of a large urban expansion project. A 1688-era bronze statue of him thus stands at its centre – the oldest equestrian statue in Scandinavia, in fact. You'll also come across a copper-clad Baroque telephone kiosk from 1913.

DET KONGELIGE TEATER

Kongens Nytorv ☎ 33 69 69 33, ⓦ kglteater
.dk. Tours (in Danish only) roughly every other
Sun 11am; 100kr. MAP PP.40–41, POCKET MAP E11

Somewhat confusingly, **Det Kongelige Teater** (the Royal Theatre) comprises three buildings: the main building on Kongens Nytorv, the Opera House on Holmen (see p.82) and the Skuespilhuset (see p.61). Built in 1874, the Kongens Nytorv theatre is by far the oldest of the three, and for years was the country's main national performance venue, hosting opera, ballet and drama under one roof – though today it is primarily used for ballet. As a fourteen-year-old, Hans Christian Andersen is known to have tried his luck as a ballet dancer here though the audition was, by all accounts, a disaster. There are occasional guided tours of the theatre, although to fully experience its grandeur you'll have to watch a performance.

Shops

BANG & OLUFSEN

Østergade 18 ☎ 33 11 14 15,
🌐 bang-olufsen.com. Mon–Thurs 10am–6pm,
Fri 10am–7pm, Sat 10am–4pm. MAP PP.40–41,
POCKET MAP D11

At B&O's sleek flagship store you can check out their latest top-of-the-range sound and vision kit: good to look at even if it might stretch beyond your holiday budget. A pair of super-lightweight headphones in funky colours will set you back 845kr.

BRUUNS BAZAAR

Kronprinsensgade 8–9 ☎ 33 32 19 99,
🌐 bruunsbazaar.dk. Mon–Fri 10am–6pm, Sat
11am–4pm. MAP PP.40–41, POCKET MAP C11

Two minimalist neighbouring stores selling simple, stylish and beautifully made clothes – ladies' at no. 8, gents' at no. 9 – created by in-house designers, hence the somewhat hefty price tag.

DAY – BIRGER ET MIKKELSEN

Pilestræde 16 ☎ 33 45 88 80, 🌐 day.dk.
Mon–Thurs 10am–6pm, Fri 10am–7pm, Sat
10am–4pm. MAP PP.40–41, POCKET MAP D11

A two-storey fashion house selling own-design women's garb with a colourful, ethnic twist. Prices from 700kr for a stripy T-shirt up to the 4500kr mark for a glittery cocktail dress.

DECADENT COPENHAGEN

Store Regnegade 3 ☎ 70 70 36 37,
🌐 decadentcopenhagen.com. Mon–Fri
11am–5.30pm, Sat 11am–4pm. MAP PP.40–41,
POCKET MAP D11

Flagship store of this Danish line, which began making high-quality, trendy yet practical leather women's handbags, and has since branched out into shoes. Bags start around 2800kr.

ECOUTURE BY LUND

Læderstræde 5 ☎ 27 58 57 30, 🌐 ecouture
.dk. Wed 2–5.30pm, Fri 2–6.30pm, 1st Sat of
month noon–4pm. MAP PP.40–41, POCKET MAP C12

You can now find the glamorous, bohemian women's clothing line with organic/socially responsible stance (hence the "eco" in the name) in a central location – although opening hours remain restricted.

GEORGE JENSEN

Amagertorv 4 ☎ 33 11 40 80, 🌐 georgejensen
.com. Mon–Fri 10am–7pm, Sat 10am–6pm,
Sun 11am–4pm. MAP PP.40–41, POCKET MAP D12

Silverware designed in the spirit and style of the celebrated silversmith Georg Jensen, who first became known for his Art Nouveau-style jewellery in the early twentieth century. A small museum inside tells his story.

HAY

Pilestræde 29–31 ☎ 42 82 08 20,
🌐 hay.dk. Mon–Fri 10am–6pm, Sat
10am–5pm. MAP PP.40–41, POCKET MAP D11

Colourful, funky household accessories, including furniture and rugs, mostly by cutting-edge Danish designers. A stunning modular sofa in grey wool will cost you 16,000kr.

HENRIK VIBSKOV

Krystalgade 6 ☎ 33 14 61 00,
ⓦ henrikvibskovboutique.com. Mon–Thurs
11am–6pm, Fri 11am–7pm, Sat 11am–5pm.
MAP PP.40–41, POCKET MAP C11

Weird and wonderful (and
pricey) gear from Copenhagen's *enfant terrible* clothes
designer. Henrik, also an artist
and drummer, is notorious for
his colourful, flamboyant and
über-trendy men's and
women's wear.

ILLUMS BOLIGHUS

Amagertorv 10 ☎ 33 14 19 41,
ⓦ illumsbolighus.dk. Mon–Fri 10am–7pm, Sat
10am–6pm, Sun 11am–5pm. MAP PP.40–41,
POCKET MAP D12

A Copenhagen institution, this
gorgeous design department
store sells everything from
top-of-the-range clothes to
furniture and kitchenware
from global designer icons. It's
also the place to go year-round
for beautiful Christmas
decorations.

JAZZCUP

Gothersgade 107 ☎ 33 33 87 40,
ⓦ jazzklubben.dk. Tues–Thurs 10am–5.30pm,
Fri 10am–6pm, Sat 10am–2pm. MAP PP.40–41,
POCKET MAP C10

Excellent music store
specializing in jazz, blues, soul
and world music. It also has a
small café and hosts regular,
intimate live shows (Fri
3.30pm, Sat 2.30pm).

KASSANDRA

Grønnegade 27 ☎ 33 91 08 89. Mon–Thurs
11am–6pm, Fri 11am–7pm, Sat 10am–4pm.
MAP PP.40–41, POCKET MAP D11

One of the most beloved shoe
stores in the city, with scores
of the latest heels from
highbrow labels that include
Jimmy Choo, Stella
McCartney, Chloé and Pedro
Garcia. Also sells bags from
the same designers.

ILLUMS BOLIGHUS

LE KLINT

Store Kirkestræde 1 ☎ 33 11 66 63,
ⓦ leklint.com. Tues–Fri 10am–6pm, Sat
10am–4pm. MAP PP.40–41, POCKET MAP D12

Originally started by famous
furniture designer Kaare Klint,
Le Klint's lamps are now a
globally sought-after brand.
The current in-house designers
have maintained his simple,
aesthetic style.

LEGO

Vimmelskaftet 37 ⓦ stores.lego.com. Mon–
Thurs & Sat 10am–6pm, Fri 10am–7pm, Sun
11am–5pm. MAP PP.40–41, POCKET MAP C12

A must for Lego connoisseurs
of all ages, the flagship store
even provides building tips
and tricks, and can get you
replacement pieces for those
crucial ones you've lost from
the colourful and never-
ending Pick-a-Brick wall.

LOUIS POULSEN

Gammel Strand 28 ☎ 70 33 14 14,
ⓦ louispoulsen.com. Mon–Thurs 8am–4pm,
Fri 8am–3.30pm. MAP PP.40–41, POCKET MAP D12

Beautiful lighting from top
designers past and present
including Poul Henningsen
whose famous glare-free PH
lamps, made up of concentric

circular metal shades, were launched in this store many moons ago.

MADS NØRGAARD

Amagertorv 13–15 ☎ 33 32 01 28, ⓦ madsnorgaard.com. Mon–Thurs 10am–6pm, Fri 10am–7pm, Sat 10am–5pm. MAP PP.40–41, POCKET MAP C12

Good-quality, own-design everyday wear for women and children (at no. 13) and men (no. 15) in cheerful, often stripy colours. Prices are reasonable for what you get.

MAGASIN DU NORD

Kongens Nytorv 13 ☎ 33 11 44 33, ⓦ magasin.dk. Daily 10am–8pm. MAP PP.40–41, POCKET MAP E12

This age-old department store is still going strong, selling top-notch clothes and homeware. Head to the basement for the gourmet food hall, well stocked with organic and fair-trade foodstuffs and wines, You'll also find magazines and newspapers from around the globe down here.

MUNTHE

Grønnegade 10 ☎ 33 32 00 12, ⓦ dk.munthe .com. Mon–Thurs 10am–6pm, Fri 10am–7pm, Sat 10am–4pm. MAP PP.40–41, POCKET MAP D11

Pricey and exciting – bordering on grungy – women's clothing, designed by Naja Munthe. Known for its exquisite details, feminine lines and high-quality materials, the collection is completely renewed every three months.

PETER BEIER CHOKOLADE

Skoubogade 1 ☎ 33 93 07 17, ⓦ pbchokolade.dk. Mon–Thurs 10am–6pm, Fri 10am–7pm, Sat 10am–5pm. MAP PP.40–41, POCKET MAP B12

Wonderful selection of handmade chocolates, made with the finest ingredients. The cocoa comes from their own plantation in the Caribbean.

ROYAL COPENHAGEN

Amagertorv 6 ☎ 33 13 71 81, ⓦ royalcopenhagen.com. Mon–Fri 10am–7pm, Sat 10am–6pm, Sun 11am–5pm. MAP PP.40–41, POCKET MAP C12

Flagship store for the Royal Porcelain Factory's famous china, distinguished by its blue patterning. The beautiful gabled store building, from 1616, is one of the city's oldest, having survived countless city-centre fires. Prices start at 299kr for a decorated egg cup.

SÖGRENI OF COPENHAGEN

Sankt Peders Stræde 30A ☎ 33 12 78 79, ⓦ sogrenibikes.com. Mon–Fri 10am–6pm, Sat 10am–4pm. MAP PP.40–41, POCKET MAP A12

Sögreni's beautiful handmade bikes are assembled in store, though with prices starting at around 12,000kr they don't come cheap. It's a great place to come and buy bike accessories, such as chain guards and lights, which are also designed and crafted in-house. Items begin at around 290kr for a pretty little copper bike bell.

PETER BEIER CHOKOLADE

SØMODS BOLCHER

Nørregade 36 ☎ 33 12 60 46, ⓦ soemods
-bolcher.dk. Mon–Thurs 9.15am–5.30pm, Fri
9.15am–6pm, Sat 10am–3.30pm, Sun
11am–3pm. MAP PP.40–41, POCKET MAP B11

Dinky little confectioner that
uses age-old methods – dating
back to its establishment in
1891 – to produce beautiful
boiled and hand-rolled candy
in myriad colours and flavours.

STIG P

Kronprinsensgade 14 ☎ 33 14 42 16,
ⓦ stigpdk. Mon–Thurs 10.30am–6pm, Fri
10.30am–7pm, Sat 10am–5pm. MAP PP.40–41,
POCKET MAP D11

This colourful, welcoming
women's clothes store was the
first to open on trendy
Kronprinsensgade, way back in
1969. Designer wear encompasses Stella McCartney, Calvin
Klein and Stig P's own label.

STILLEBEN

Niels Hemmingsensgade 3 ☎ 33 91 11 31,
ⓦ stilleben.dk. Mon–Fri 10am–6pm, Sat
10am–5pm. MAP PP.40–41, POCKET MAP C12

Funky ceramics, glass, textiles
and much, much more from
mostly Danish designers. They
seem to specialize in quirky
items that, once seen, you'll
never be able to live without.

STILLEBEN

Cafés and restaurants

ATLAS BAR

Larsbjørnsstræde 18 ☎ 33 15 03 52,
ⓦ atlasbar.dk. Mon–Sat noon–10pm.
MAP PP.40–41, POCKET MAP B12

Informal café-cum-restaurant
serving affordable dishes from
around the globe in a
charming, laidback setting.
There is an extensive
vegetarian menu (including
delicious nut burgers made
with hazelnuts, carrots and
celeriac; 135kr/160kr for
lunch/dinner) with a good
range of freshly made salads,
and lots of freshly squeezed
juices, too.

BAR'VIN

Skindergade 3 ☎ 33 12 58 03, ⓦ barvin.dk.
Mon–Thurs 11.30am–11pm, Fri–Sat
11.30am–midnight. MAP PP.40–41, POCKET MAP C11

The menu at this rustic,
relaxed wine bar changes to
match the wine (rather than
the other way around), though
the delicious charcuterie and
cheese platters always remain
a good bet. Expect to pay
from 85kr for a sandwich and
up to 395kr for a three-course
meal.

CAFÉ HOVEDTELEGRAFEN

Købmagergade 37 ☎ 33 41 09 86,
ⓦ cafehovedtelegrafen.dk. Daily 10am–4pm.
MAP PP.40–41, POCKET MAP C11

With great views across the
city spires, this bright and airy
café-restaurant on the top
floor of the Post & Tele
Museum serves smørrebrød to
die for (from 99kr), as well as
excellent salads and well-made
sandwiches. When the weather
is good enough there is also
outdoor seating on the
balcony.

EUROPA 1989

CONDITORI LA GLACE

Skoubogade 3 ☎ 33 14 46 46, ⓦ laglace.dk.
Mon–Fri 8.30am–6pm, Sat 9am–6pm, Sun
10am–6pm (closed Sun April–Sept). MAP
PP.40–41, POCKET MAP B12

Traditional patisserie serving
beautifully crafted layer cakes
and pastries. Try the scrumptious HC Hat cake, made with
chocolate, caramel mousse and
lemon ganache (57kr per slice).

DALLE VALLE

Fiolstræde 3–5 ☎ 33 93 29 29,
ⓦ cafedallevalle.dk. Mon–Sat 10am–midnight,
Sun 10am–11pm. MAP PP.40–41, POCKET MAP B11

This spacious, bustling café is a
great place for sandwiches and
salads, with a few pasta dishes,
burgers and steaks also on offer;
scrummy hot wings, too (all
around 100–130kr). Also a
popular bar at night, with a DJ
on Friday and Saturday.

DET LILLE APOTEK

Store Kannikestræde 15 ☎ 33 12 56 06,
ⓦ detlilleapotek.dk. Daily 11.30am–midnight.
MAP PP.40–41, POCKET MAP C11

Dating back to 1720, the city's
oldest restaurant was once one
of Hans Christian Andersen's
favourite haunts, and with its
leadlight windows and hanging
oil lamps it still retains plenty of
old-time atmosphere. Highlights
on the menu of traditional
Danish dishes include *biksemad*

(beef stew served with pickled
beetroot, cucumber salad, fried
eggs and slices of rye bread;
98kr) for lunch and *flæskesteg*
(pork roast with crackling,
sugar-glazed potatoes, pickled
red cabbage and a thick, creamy
sauce; 169kr) for dinner.

EUROPA 1989

Amagertorv 1 ☎ 33 14 28 89, ⓦ europa1989
.dk. Mon–Thurs 7.45am–11pm, Fri & Sat
7.45am–midnight, Sun 9am–10pm. MAP
PP.40–41, POCKET MAP D12

Large, fancy café on bustling
Højbro Plads serving excellent
coffee and cake, good breakfasts
(wholegrain porridge 39kr) and
brunch (daily until 3pm; 149kr).
It's also a popular after-work
spot, mostly for the drinks (the
beer selection is good) and their
excellent nibbles; try the
shellfish bisque or *bruschetta*.

KONG HANS KÆLDER

Vingårdstræde 6 ☎ 33 11 68 68,
ⓦ konghans.dk. Mon–Sat 6pm–midnight.
MAP PP.40–41, POCKET MAP D12

Set in the cellar of a medieval
merchant's house, this
Michelin-starred place has a
setting as dramatic as it is
romantic. The picture-perfect
food is French-inspired with a
twist. The eight-course menu
will set you back a mere 1400kr,
not including wine, while an à la
carte main starts at 550kr.

KROGS FISKERESTAURANT

Gammel Strand 38 ☎ 33 15 89 15, ⓦ krogs
.dk. Open for lunch and dinner, check website
for details. MAP PP.40–41, POCKET MAP C12

Though hidden behind the
metro building chaos, the
grande dame of the city's
seafood restaurants – all high
ceilings and meticulously
dressed tables – is worth the
hassle to get to. Half a dozen
French oysters will set you back
a couple of hundred kroner, or
– if you're feeling flush – try the
lobster with all the trimmings.

LA GALETTE

Larsbjørnsstræde 9 ☎ 33 32 37 90,
ⓦ lagalette.dk. Mon–Sat noon–4pm &
5.30–10pm, Sun 1–10pm. MAP PP.40–41,
POCKET MAP B12

Informal place serving
French-style buckwheat
pancakes with both sweet and
savoury fillings. Specialities
include the Menez-Hom (90kr),
filled with goat's cheese, walnuts
and salad, and the Normande
(60kr) with calvados-flambéed
caramelized apples. In summer
there's outdoor seating in the
back yard.

L'EDUCATION NATIONALE

Larsbjørnsstræde 12 ☎ 33 91 53 60,
ⓦ leducation.dk. Mon–Sat 11.30am–midnight,
Sun 4.30–10pm. MAP PP.40–41, POCKET MAP B12

Authentic and cosy, French-
style bistro with tightly packed
tables and French-speaking
waiters. Lunchtime standards,
such as omelette (85kr) and
moules marinières (89kr), are
very reasonably priced. The
evening menu is pricier but still
good value (mains such as
pheasant or sea bass around
200kr), and there's an excellent
selection of wines.

MAVEN

Nikolaj Plads 10 ☎ 32 20 11 00,
ⓦ restaurantmaven.dk. Mon–Thurs
11.30am–midnight, Fri & Sat 11.30am–2am.
MAP PP.40–41, POCKET MAP B12

Inside the massive, red-brick
Skt Nikolaj Kirke, a deconse-
crated church that also hosts
temporary exhibitions, *Maven*
("stomach") offers excellent
French/Italian-inspired lunch
and dinner menus as well as
traditional lunchtime
smørrebrød (198kr for a
platter). Also a popular spot for
evening drinks.

NORDEN

Østergade 61 ☎ 33 11 77 91, ⓦ cafenorden
.dk. Daily 8.30am–midnight. MAP PP.40–41,
POCKET MAP B12

A great pit stop on busy Strøget
with fabulous home-made
cakes and pancakes as well as
beautifully assembled salads
(from 165kr). There's also a fine
selection of beer (including
from the Jacobsen brewery; see
p.89), a range of cocktails and a
good few wines.

OLIVER AND THE BLACK CIRCUS

Teglgårdsstræde 8A ☎ 74 56 88 88,
ⓦ oliverandtheblackcircus.com. Tues–Sat
5.30pm–midnight. MAP PP.40–41, POCKET MAP B11

Dark and moody yet cosy, this
eccentric and bohemian new
restaurant decor (check out
the goblins) offers fabulous
starter-sized dishes – such as
cured mackerel and blueber-
ries or cod roe and bacon –
which you can mix and match
to create your own menu
(three/four/five courses
330/415/480kr).

PALUDAN BOGCAFÉ

Fiolstræde 10–12 ☎ 33 15 06 75,
ⓦ paludan-cafe.dk. Mon–Fri 9am–10pm,
Sat–Sun 10am–10pm. MAP PP.40–41, POCKET
MAP B11

With its free wi-fi and
great-value meals – chicken
tagliatelle (89kr) or the
Paludan burger, for example
– this bookshop-cum-café is

a great student hangout. There's also good coffee and cheap beer.

PEDER OXE

Gråbrødretorv 11 ☎ 33 11 00 77, ⓦ pederoxe .dk. Mon–Wed & Sun 11.30am–10.30pm Thurs–Sat 11.30am–11pm. MAP PP.40–41. POCKET MAP C11

One of several cafés and restaurants on this historic square (once home to a Greyfriars monastery), serving juicy, grilled organic burgers (from 145kr) and steaks (200kr) plus unlimited salads (95kr). The "dessert tapas" platter (140kr) is an exquisite experience in itself. Also a good place to go for drinks.

PILEKÆLDEREN

Pilestræde 48 ☎ 33 33 00 26, ⓦ pilekaelderen .dk. Mon–Sat 11.30am–5pm. MAP PP.40–41. POCKET MAP D11

Authentic, traditional lunchtime restaurant with thick stone walls and a low wood-beamed ceiling. It specializes in stunning smørrebrød, such as herring marinated in elderberry aquavit (68kr) – all home-made, of course.

ROYAL CAFÉ

Amagertorv 6 ☎ 33 12 11 22, ⓦ royalsmushicafe .dk. Mon–Sat 10am–7pm, Sun 10am–6pm, Sun 11am–5pm. MAP PP.40–41, POCKET MAP C12

In the courtyard of the Royal Copenhagen flagship store, the *Royal Café* is the originator of "smushi" (meaning sushi smørrebrød), with a selection that changes with the seasons. Try a platter of three smushi (139kr) or sample individual pieces for 48kr. Most locals consider these to be the best modern takes on smørrebrød in town. It can get very crowded, especially on weekends, so you might have to ask for your smushi to go.

SLOTSKÆLDEREN HOS GITTE KIK

Fortunstræde 4 ☎ 33 11 15 37, ⓦ slotskaelderen.dk. Tues–Sat 10am–5pm. MAP PP.40–41, POCKET MAP D12

Cosy basement restaurant serving excellent traditional smørrebrød. Choose from the vast selection at the counter, such as delicious *rullepølse* (rolled pork with parsley and pepper), and the food will be brought to your table.

ROYAL CAFÉ

BO-BI BAR

SULT

Vognmagergade 8B ☎ 33 74 34 17,
ⓦ restaurantsult.dk. Tues–Fri noon–10pm, Sat
& Sun 9am–10pm. MAP PP.40–41, POCKET MAP C10
Occupying a high-ceilinged
dining hall in the same building
as the Danish Film Institute,
Sult does simple well-prepared
Danish dishes that don't cost the
earth. Try the mouthwatering
freshly cured ham from Jutland,
served with grilled tomatoes
and artichokes (129kr).

VANDKUNSTEN SANDWICH & SALATBAR

Rådhusstræde 17 ☎ 33 13 90 40,
ⓦ vsandwich.dk. Mon–Sat 10am–4pm.
MAP PP.40–41, POCKET MAP C12
Excellent place to grab a
sandwich on the go (39–52kr),
with lots of yummy vegetarian
options (avocado mousse,
mozzarella and so on) and
freshly baked, crisp Italian
rolls. Salads, which you can
make up yourself, start at 44kr.

Bars

1105

Kristen Bernikows Gade 4 ☎ 33 93 11 05,
ⓦ 1105.dk. Wed, Thurs & Sat 8pm–2am, Fri
4pm–2am. MAP PP.40–41, POCKET MAP D11
Cool, elegant, low-lit cocktail
bar, where the mixologists wear

crisp white lab coats. *1105* has
made a name for itself with the
creation of the Copenhagen
cocktail, a delicious mix of
genever (Dutch gin), cherry
liqueur, lime juice and a host of
secret ingredients.

BO-BI BAR

Klareboderne 4 ☎ 33 12 55 43. Daily
noon–2am. MAP PP.40–41, POCKET MAP C11
This Baroque, red hole-in-the-
wall is one of the city's most
authentic watering holes.
Opened in 1917, it sports
Copenhagen's oldest bar
counter and attracts a
refreshingly boho clientele of
writers, students and
intellectuals – great for
people-watching. Serves cheap
bottles of great Danish and
Czech beers as well as local
schnapps.

CHARLIE'S BAR

Pilestræde 33 ☎ 33 22 22 89. Mon 2pm–
midnight, Tues & Wed noon–1am,
Thurs–Sat noon–2am, Sun 2–11pm.
MAP PP.40–41, POCKET MAP D11
Packed, small and smoky,
Copenhagen's only UK-style
pub – even boasting Casque
Mark accreditation – draws in
the crowds night after night for
its ever-changing range of
British ales and ciders.

K-BAR

Ved Stranden 20 ☎ 33 91 92 22, ⓦ k-bar.dk.
Mon–Thurs 4pm–1am, Fri & Sat 4pm–2am. MAP
PP.40–41, POCKET MAP D12

Tucked away around the corner
from Højbro Plads, this funky
cocktail bar has deep, cosy
sofas into which punters can
happily sink as they sip the
beautiful concoctions of owner
Kirsten – hence the K. Try the
unusual and very moreish
Rissitini, made with gin, sake,
lychee liqueur and ginger.

THE LIVING ROOM

Larsbjørnsstræde 17 ☎ 33 32 66 10.
Mon–Thurs 9am–11pm, Fri 9am–2am, Sat
10am–2am, Sun noon–7pm. MAP PP.40–41,
POCKET MAP B12

Laidback corner bar on chilled
Larsbjørnsstræde, with tables
outside and soft sofas in the
basement. It's a great place to
go for freshly squeezed juices,
organic wines, coffee and
affordable cocktails.

RUBY

Nybrogade 10 ☎ 33 93 12 03, ⓦ rby.dk.
Mon–Sat 4pm–2am, Sun 7pm–2am.
MAP PP.40–41, POCKET MAP C12

Set in what appears to be for all
the world an unassuming
ground-floor apartment, with
comfy leather armchairs and
no obvious signage, this is
possibly the city's best cocktail
bar. Try the signature
Rapscallion – a Scottish take on
the Manhattan, with Talisker
over a sweet PX sherry.

ZEN

Nørregade 41 ⓦ zen.dk. Thurs–Sat
11pm–4am. MAP PP.40–41, POCKET MAP B11

This chic, exclusive nightclub is
run by Denmark's answer to
Simon Cowell, meaning one
thing: fat beats, pretty young
things grinding on the
dance-floor and oodles of
pretension. Go, if you must.

Music venues

DROP INN

Kompagnistræde 34 ☎ 33 11 24 04,
ⓦ drop-inn.dk. Mon–Thurs 2pm–2am, Fri–Sat
noon–5am. Usually free Mon–Thurs; Fri & Sat
from 30kr. MAP PP.40–41, POCKET MAP B12

Small folk, blues and rock
venue, with tables spilling onto
the pavement during hot
summer months and a good
selection of international
beers. Music from 10/10.30pm
most nights (usually free
during the week; from 30kr Sat
& Sun).

JAZZHUS MONTMARTRE

Store Regnegade 19A ☎ 70 26 32 67,
ⓦ jazzhusmontmartre.dk. Doors open at
5.30pm. MAP PP.40–41, POCKET MAP D11

Intimate, not-for-profit jazz
club, which reopened in 2010
after having placed Copenhagen
firmly on the international jazz
map in the 1950s when it
hosted legends such as Dexter
Gordon and Stan Getz.
Concerts two to three nights a
week (100–350kr).

LA FONTAINE

Kompagnistræde 11 ☎ 33 11 60 98,
ⓦ lafontaine.dk. Daily 7pm–5am.
MAP PP.40–41, POCKET MAP C12

As Copenhagen's oldest jazz
venue, *La Fontaine* has for
decades been where jazz
musicians make for on their
nights off. It's small and packed,
with live gigs at the weekend
(Fri–Sat from 10pm, Sun from
9pm; entry from 70kr).

MUSIKCAFÉEN

Rådhusstræde 13 ☎ 21 51 21 51,
ⓦ huset-kbh.dk. MAP PP.40–41, POCKET MAP C12

On the third floor of the Huset
cultural centre, this is the place
to hear up-and-coming bands
before they become famous.
Gigs most nights, starting at 8
or 9pm (40–150kr).

Slotsholmen

Encircled by Indre By on three sides and abutting the Inner Harbour on the fourth, the flat, diminutive island of Slotsholmen has been the country's seat of power for almost a thousand years. It was here, in 1167, that Bishop Absalon founded a castle to protect the village's herring traders from Wendish pirates. The area is anchored by the commanding and glum-looking Christiansborg Slot; home to the Danish parliament and the royals' reception rooms, it's the fifth incarnation of a royal dwelling on this site. Other highlights within the palace complex include the extravagant Royal Stables and riding ground, the elegant Palace Chapel and, next door, the colourful Thorvald-sens Museum, while on the opposite side of Christiansborg the Daniel Libeskind-designed interior of the Danish Jewish Museum and, on the waterfront, the gleaming Black Diamond extension to the Royal Library provide more modern architectural draws.

FOLKETING (DANISH PARLIAMENT)

Christiansborg ☎ 33 37 32 21, ⓦ thedanishparliament.dk. Tours (free) most Sundays at 1pm (tickets available from 10am and online). Sittings roughly Oct to mid-June: Tues & Wed from 1pm, Thurs & Fri from 10am. MAP OPPOSITE, POCKET MAP D13

Occupying the southern half of the three-winged palace of Christiansborg, the **Folketing** (Danish parliament) is a must for fans of the cult TV political drama series *Borgen*, set in and around the palace. You can watch the debates in the principal parliamentary chamber, the **Folketingssal**, when in session – ring the visitors' entrance bell, and, if spaces are available, you'll be taken through security checks to the public galleries – though bear in mind that debates are not nearly as animated as the UK equivalent. Alternatively the Sunday English-language **tours** cover the history of Danish

democracy as well as the palace's colourful history, taking you down the long Vandrehal where the much revered original Danish constitution from 1849 is displayed in a silver chest.

ROYAL RECEPTION ROOMS

Christiansborg ☎ 33 92 64 92, ⓦ christiansborg.dk. May–Sept daily 10am–5pm; Oct–April Tues–Sun 10am–5pm; closed during royal functions. 80kr, 120kr for combined ticket with Ruins under Christiansborg and Royal Stables. Tours at 3pm. MAP OPPOSITE, POCKET MAP D12

Although it was built as a royal palace, the royals have never actually lived at Christiansborg, favouring the slightly more open and accessible Amalienborg. A section of the northern wing of the palace is, however, still in royal use for official functions as the **Royal Reception Rooms** (Det Kongelige Repræsentation-slokaler) accessed via the Inner Courtyard. Sure to impress any visiting dignitaries, all the rooms

are beautifully adorned. An intricate marble frieze depicting Alexander's march into Babylon by Thorvaldsen (see p.55) was recovered from the previous Christiansborg and following skilful restoration is on display in the Alexander Hall. The marble walls in the oval Throne Room are clad in delicate silks from Lyon, while on the ceiling a magnificent painting depicts

the origins of the national flag. Best of all, however, is the long Great Hall, lined with seventeen magnificent tapestries by Bjørn Nørgaard (also famous for the mosaics on Strøget; see p.41). A fiftieth birthday present for the current Queen, they depict the country's history from the Viking Age to the present. See if you can spot The Beatles and Mao Zedong.

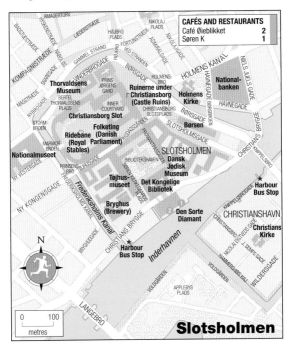

CAFÉS AND RESTAURANTS	
Café Øieblikket	2
Søren K	1

Slotsholmen

RUINERNE UNDER CHRISTIANSBORG (CASTLE RUINS)

Christiansborg ☎ 33 92 64 92, ⓦ christiansborg.dk. Daily 10am–5pm (closed Mon Oct–April). Tours Sat at noon. 50kr, 120kr for combined ticket with Royal Reception Rooms and Royal Stables.MAP P.53, POCKET MAP D12

The **ruins** of Slotsholmen's two earliest castles have been excavated and now form part of an underground **exhibition** beneath Christiansborg, accessed via a stairwell from the main entrance portal. A walkway tracks the foundations of Bishop Absalon's original castle, while the extant highlight of its successor, Københavns Slot, which was put up in the late fourteenth century, is the foundations of its notorious Blue Tower prison where King Christian IV's daughter Leonora Christine was kept captive for 22 years, supposedly due to her blinding beauty.

RIDEBANE (ROYAL STABLES)

Christiansborg Ridebane 12 ☎ 33 92 64 92, ⓦ christiansborg.dk. May–Sept daily 1.30–4pm; Oct–April Tues–Sun 1.30–4pm. Tours in English Sat at 2pm. 50kr, 120kr for combined ticket with Royal Reception Rooms and Ruins under Christiansborg. MAP P.53, POCKET MAP C13

Beyond the Inner Courtyard, the **Ridebane** (Royal Stables) and surrounding riding ground are all that's left of the opulent Baroque palace that stood here from 1738 until it burnt to the ground 56 years later. If you arrive around mid-morning you stand a good chance of seeing the Queen's horses being exercised either in the outdoor riding arena, or, if you poke your head in discreetly, in the lavish Riding Hall.

The **Museet Kongelige Stalde og Kareter** (Museum of Royal Stables and Coaches), in the southern flank, houses the extravagant marble-clad stables where a few lucky horses are still kept, alongside the royal collection of gilded carriages plus the previous king's beautiful old Bentley.

To the west as you exit the museum, the Baroque **Marmorbroen** (Marble Bridge) linking Slotsholmen with mainland Indre By was the original palace's main approach.

CHRISTIANSBORG SLOTSKIRKE (PALACE CHAPEL)

Prins Jørgens Gård 1 ⓦ christiansborg.dk. July daily 10am–5pm; Aug–June Sun 10am–5pm. Tours in Danish Sun at 2pm. MAP P.53, POCKET MAP D12

Fully restored following a catastrophic fire in 1992 the Neoclassical **Palace Chapel** is all that remains of the second Christiansborg palace, which like its predecessor also burnt to the ground some fifty-odd years after completion (in 1833). The palace was said to be the most lavish of all the Christiansborg incarnations, though the church's elegant and light interior – topped by a vast white dome with four angels in

ROYAL STABLES

Royalty Danish style

The Danish Royal Family stands as one of the oldest monarchies in the world. The current monarch, Her Majesty Queen Margrethe II, traces her lineage all the way back to Harald Bluetooth, the famous Viking chieftain and first king of a united Denmark over a thousand years ago. The Royal Family remains an extremely popular institution in Denmark. Crown Prince Frederik has been regularly voted "Dane of The Year", while his Tasmanian-born wife Princess Mary,

a relaxed mum of four, is both vaunted style icon and global advocate of women's health. In April 2015, the 75th birthday of Queen Margrethe – who will celebrate 45 years on the throne in 2017 – was honoured with a round of gala dinners attended by royals from across Europe.

relief seemingly floating beneath – is exquisite Classical simplicity itself. Still put to use for the opening of parliament service and for the occasional royal event, such as the baptism of the Crown Prince's first child in 2006, the church is also used for organ practice by the Danish Music Conservatory.

THORVALDSENS MUSEUM

Bertel Thorvaldsens Plads 2 ☎ 33 32 15 32, ⓦ thorvaldsensmuseum.dk. Tues–Sun 10am–5pm. 40kr. MAP P.53, POCKET MAP C12

Dedicated to Denmark's most internationally celebrated sculptor, the **Thorvaldsens Museum** is an absorbing place to while away a few hours. You certainly won't miss the grand Neoclassical edifice, overlooking the picturesque Frederiksholms Kanal, within which it's housed: with its striking ochre facade, and unusual slanting doors and window frames, it stands out as one of the city's most original buildings.

Having trained in Copenhagen, **Bertel Thorvaldsen** (1770–1844) spent forty years fulfilling high-profile commissions in Rome before returning triumphantly in 1839 – an event depicted on the huge frieze painted on the canal-facing side of the building. Thorvaldsen spent the last few years of his life fulfilling commissions in Copenhagen, and his work can be seen in both Vor Frue Kirke and Christiansborg Slotskirke.

Inside, richly decorated walls and mosaic floors provide a fitting backdrop for the vast collection of Thorvaldsen's works on the ground floor, from huge marble sculptures to sketches and grubby plaster casts with the sculptor's own original marks. Highlights include the intimate *Cupid and Psyche* and Thorvaldsen's own self-portrait in stone. Upstairs, the sculptor's fine collection of Greek, Roman and Egyptian antiquities is on display.

TØJHUSMUSEET

Tøjhusgade 2 ☎ 41 20 63 72, ⓦ thm.dk.
Tues–Sun noon–4pm. Free. MAP P.53,
POCKET MAP D13

Whether you're a fan of weapons or not, the **Tøjhusmuseet** (Royal Danish Arsenal Museum), occupying the arsenal of the old Copenhagen Castle (a forerunner of Christiansborg), is a treasure-trove for arms buffs. There are rows and rows of swords and firearms on display. Most remarkable, though, is the 156m arched hall housing the cannon collection, said to be the longest such hall in Europe.

BØRSEN

Børsgade. MAP P.53, POCKET MAP D13

A fanciful riot of gables, pinnacles and grey-green copper, the red-brick **Børsen** building is one of the more remarkable monuments of Christian IV's reign. It's for its wonderfully whimsical spire – made up of the intertwined tails of four sculpted dragons – that the building is best known. The dragons supposedly protect the Børsen from attack and fire, and seem to be fulfilling their duties quite successfully as the building has survived many a skirmish as those around it have burnt to the ground. Although ownership of the building has long since passed to the Chamber of Commerce (it's not open to the public), the dragon spire remains the official symbol of the Danish stock exchange.

DANSK JØDISK MUSEUM

Proviantpassagen 6 ☎ 33 11 22 18,
ⓦ jewmus.dk. June–Aug Tues–Sun
10am–5pm; Sept–May Tues–Fri 1–4pm, Sat &
Sun noon–5pm. 50kr for one exhibit; 75kr for
multiple exhibits. MAP P.53, POCKET MAP D13

Opened in 2004 and designed by Daniel Libeskind, architect of the new World Trade Center site in New York, the **Danish Jewish Museum** retells the story of Jewry in Denmark from their arrival in the seventeenth century at the invitation of Christian IV up to the gruesome wartime period. Housed in the Galajhus (Royal Boat House), the building gives no indication from the outside of its subtly disorientating interior, a labyrinth of fractured passageways and sloping floors reminiscent of Libeskind's more famous Jewish Museum in Berlin. The museum's layout corresponds to the interlocking characters of the Hebrew word *Mitzvah* ("good deed"), a reference to the Danes' smuggling of seven thousand Jews hidden away in fishing boats across to sanctuary in Sweden during World War II (see box, p.62).

The exhibition itself is divided into five sections, focusing on different aspects of Danish-Jewish life. The most captivating of these is the Mitzvah section itself, which recounts the plight of Danish Jews during Nazi occupation. There are some

DANSK JØDISK MUSEUM

heartfelt and touching letters and photos from refugees in Sweden on show, and hand-drawn sketches of horrible episodes at the Theresienstadt concentration camp (in what's now the Czech Republic), where 481 Danish Jews were sent.

DEN SORTE DIAMANT (THE BLACK DIAMOND)

Søren Kierkegaards Plads 1 ☎ 33 47 47 47, ⓦ kb.dk. Mon–Sat 8am–9pm. Access to all museums 40kr. Tours Sat 3pm 60kr (including access to all museums). MAP P.53, POCKET MAP D13

Den Sorte Diamant (The Black Diamond), a monumental slab of black Zimbabwean granite and glass that leans over (and glitters magically in) the waters of the Inner Harbour below, is one of the city's great modern architectural icons. Completed in 1999, the building is an extension to the Italian-inspired **Kongelige Bibliotek** (Royal Library) (1906), to which it is connected by a futuristic glass-enclosed bridge.

The building houses an auditorium with outstanding acoustics, museums dedicated to photography and cartoon art, and a changing display of works from the Royal Library's collection. You're free to wander about the building at will, though some of the exhibitions (see below) do charge an entrance fee. Among its attractions are the National Museum of Photography, which – in addition to some 50,000 photos in its collection, dating back to the birth of photography in 1839 – hosts interesting changing exhibitions of both modern and historical photographers (Mon–Sat 10am–7pm; 40kr).

The old library building behind is less accessible to the general public and best experienced on the **guided tours**, which take in both buildings. Highlights of the Royal Library include several of the atmospheric old study halls, one which features the city's earliest grid-powered electric lamps.

Café and restaurant

CAFÉ ØIEBLIKKET

Søren Kierkegaards Plads 1 ☎ 33 47 41 06, ⓦ oieblikket.dk. Mon–Fri 8am–7pm, Sat 9am–6pm. MAP P.53, POCKET MAP D13

A popular venue among the city's studious, this café, located in the light and airy foyer of the Black Diamond, serves excellent coffee and a tempting array of mouthwatering cakes. There are deckchairs on the Inner Harbour quayside in summer, too.

SØREN K

Kierkegaards Plads 1 ☎ 33 47 49 49, ⓦ soerenk.dk. Mon–Sat noon–4pm & 5.30–10pm. MAP P.53, POCKET MAP D13

Immaculate and minimalist, the Black Diamond's upmarket waterfront restaurant boasts beautifully dressed tables lined up along the quayside walkway. It's packed throughout the day, with champagne and oysters (120kr) the lunchtime favourite, while in the evenings there's a five-course menu (435kr) focused around local produce. *Borgen* fans will notice that this is where many of PM Birgitte Nyborg's external meetings take place.

Nyhavn and Frederiksstaden

Packed with busy bars and restaurants, canalside Nyhavn attracts thousands of visitors thanks to its pretty postcard setting. To its north are the elegant Rococo houses and immaculately straight streets of Frederiksstaden, built as a grand symbol of Frederik V's reign. The huge dome of the Marmorkirken dominates the skyline, while three main north–south streets divide the area: Store Kongensgade, lined with galleries, restaurants and high-end shops; quieter Bredgade; and partially cobbled Amaliegade, which bisects the palaces of Amalienborg – the royals' official winter residence. All three streets lead up to Christian IV's impressive defensive fortress, the grass-bastioned Kastellet, close to which is a pair of inspirational museums. Finally, perched on a lonely rock off the Kastellet's northern edge, is the city's most famous icon – the diminutive Little Mermaid.

NYHAVN

MAP OPPOSITE, POCKET MAP E11–F11

Picturesque **Nyhavn** is perhaps the city's most popular tourist hangout. The "new harbour" was created in 1671 to link Kongens Nytorv to the sea – the earliest of the townhouses, no. 9, dates from this period – and has been home to some famous residents – Hans Christian Andersen lived for a while at no. 67. The area has not always been so salubrious, however: Nyhavn went through a long period as the city's most disreputable red-light district before its transformation into the welcoming visitor haunt of today. On a sunny summer's evening (there are outdoor heaters in winter) it's easy to see the attraction of sipping a beer while gazing over the historic yachts (usually) moored in the harbour. Be warned, though: food and drink do not come cheap.

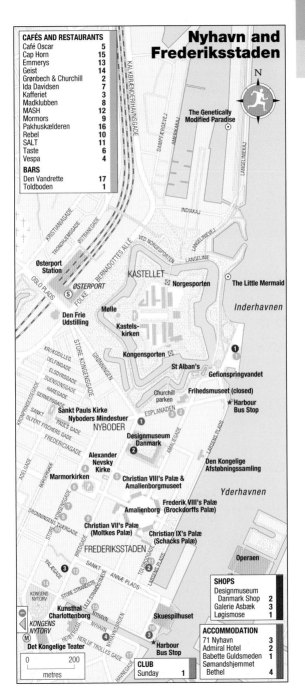

Nyhavn and Frederiksstaden

N

CAFÉS AND RESTAURANTS

Café Oscar	5
Cap Horn	15
Emmerys	13
Geist	14
Grønbech & Churchill	2
Ida Davidsen	7
Kafferiet	3
Madklubben	8
MASH	12
Mormors	9
Pakhuskælderen	16
Rebel	10
SALT	11
Taste	6
Vespa	4

BARS

Den Vandrette	17
Toldboden	1

The Genetically
Modified Paradise

INDIAKAJ

Østerport
Station

ØSTERPORT

KASTELLET

Norgesporten

The Little Mermaid

Inderhavnen

Den Frie
Udstilling

Mølle

Kastels-
kirken

Kongensporten

St Alban's

Gefionspringvandet

Frihedsmuseet (closed)

★ Harbour
Bus Stop

Sankt Pauls Kirke
Nyboders Mindestuer

Churchill
parken

NYBODER

ESPLANADEN

Designmuseum
Danmark

Alexander
Nevsky
Kirke

Den Kongelige
Afstøbningssamling

Marmorkirken

Christian VIII's Palæ &
Amalienborgmuseet

Frederik VIII's Palæ
Amalienborg (Brockdorffs Palæ)

Yderhavnen

Christian VII's Palæ
(Moltkes Palæ)

Christian IX's Palæ
(Schacks Palæ)

FREDERIKSSTADEN

Operaen

KONGENS
NYTORV

Kunsthal
Charlottenborg

Skuespilhuset

KONGENS
NYTORV

Det Kongelige Teater

★ Harbour
Bus Stop

0	200

metres

SHOPS

Designmuseum Danmark Shop	2
Galerie Asbæk	3
Løgismose	1

ACCOMMODATION

71 Nyhavn	3
Admiral Hotel	2
Babette Guldsmeden	1
Sømandshjemmet Bethel	4

CLUB

Sunday	1

59

AMALIENBORG

KUNSTHAL CHARLOTTENBORG

Nyhavn 2 ☎ 33 74 46 39, ⓦ charlottenborg
.dk. Tues & Thurs–Sun 11am–5pm, Wed
11am–8pm; 40kr. MAP P.59, POCKET MAP E11

Located between Kongens
Nytorv and Nyhavn (and with
entrances on both) the **Kunsthal
Charlottenborg** is housed in
one of the least prepossessing
palaces in Copenhagen. Built for
the illegitimate son of Frederik
III, it has since 1754 been home
to the Royal Danish Academy of
Fine Arts. There are no
permanent displays but
changing exhibitions of modern
art are put on in the newer
building (added in 1883)
behind. One such exhibition
in 1971, about the new hippie
movement, triggered the
founding of Christiania
(see p.80).

AMALIENBORG

MAP P.59, POCKET MAP F10

The winter residence of the
Danish royal family, **Amalienborg** is made up four almost
identical Rococo palaces,
arranged symmetrically around
an octagonal courtyard that
centres on a statue of Frederik
V on horseback. Designed by
royal architect Nicolai Eigtved

in 1750, the palaces were
originally built for (and funded
by) wealthy Danish nobles,
though the royals comman-
deered them following the
devastating fire at Christiansborg in 1794. Today all four
palaces are named both after
their original benefactor and a
subsequent resident royal. The
Queen lives in Christian IX's
Palæ – or Schacks Palæ – with
her husband Prince Henrik,
while Frederik VIII's Palæ
(Brockdorffs Palæ) is home to
Crown Prince Frederik and
family; both are completely
off-limits.

Note too that **Christian VII's
Palæ** (also known as Moltkes
Palæ), whose fabulous Great
Hall is considered to be one of
the finest Rococo rooms in
Europe, is unfortunately no
longer open to the public.

You can, however, visit
Christian VIII's Palæ
(Levetzaus Palæ), the first floor
of which contains the
Amalienborgmuseet
(Amalienborg Museum; May–
Oct daily 10am–4pm; Nov–
April Tues–Sun 11am–4pm;
90kr; ⓦ amalienborgmuseet
.dk), devoted to more recent
royal history. The studies of

each of the last three kings have been fully reconstructed (complete with vast pipe collections and family portraits), giving a flavour of their modern if by no means luxurious lifestyles.

Outside on the courtyard, the **changing of the guard** ceremony at noon each day is a great hit with kids. Childish souls may try to see if they can induce the bearskin-wearing guard to flinch – chances are they won't.

SKUESPILHUSET

Sankt Annæ Plads 36 ☎ 33 69 69 33, ⓦ kglteater.dk. Guided tours (75min) 100kr; check website for times. MAP P.59, POCKET MAP F11

Completed in 2008, the **Skuespilhuset** (Playhouse), around the corner from Nyhavn, is unanimously agreed to be one of the city's most elegant new buildings. It has a stunning position on the Inner Harbour, with a projecting upper storey that appears to be balancing precariously over the water's edge. A copper-clad tower thrusts skyward from within, while a wooden promenade encircles the building and doubles as an outdoor café. To see the inside, either join one of the irregular tours or take in a performance – although productions here are almost exclusively staged in Danish.

MARMORKIRKEN

Frederiksgade 4 ☎ 33 15 01 44. Mon–Thurs & Sat 10am–5pm, Fri & Sun noon–5pm. Free. MAP P.59, POCKET MAP E10

Modelled on St Peter's in the Vatican, the **Marmorkirken** (Marble Church), which is properly called Frederiks Kirke, took almost 150 years to complete. Originally commissioned by Frederik V in 1749,

the church's construction was halted twenty years later due to lack of funds, and only with financial support from a leading Danish industrial magnate, C.F. Tietgen, was it completed – using cheaper marble – in 1894, having languished in ruins for more than a century. Though the exterior is largely hidden behind scaffolding until 2017, you can still access the massive interior, dominated by a colossal **dome** some 31m in diameter. If you arrive at the right time (Aug daily 1pm & 3pm; Sept–July Sat & Sun 1pm & 3pm; 25kr), you can join a tour to climb the 260 steps to the top of the **dome**, from which there are spectacular views down over diminutive Copenhagen beneath you and towards the Swedish coastline in the distance. Note too how the relatively new Operaen across the harbour has been aligned perfectly with the Marmorkirken and Amalienborg.

MARMORKIRKEN INTERIOR

DESIGNMUSEUM DANMARK

Bredgade 68 ☎ 33 18 56 56, ⓦ designmuseum
.dk. Tues & Thurs–Sun 11am–5pm, Wed
11am–9pm. 100kr. MAP P.59, POCKET MAP G6

Formerly the Kunstindustri-museet, and not to be confused with the (now closed) Danish Design Center, this temple to (predominantly Danish) design occupies the four wings of the old Frederiks Hospital. Pride of place among the permanent exhibitions goes to the section on twentieth-century **Danish applied art and craft**, which takes in the full range of the iconic designs that have given Denmark its international reputation – from Arne Jacobsen's Ant chair to Kaj Bojesen's classic wooden toy monkey and Ole Kirk Christiansen's Lego brick. Elsewhere, the collection traces the history of European and Asian applied and decorative art, with the emphasis on how it relates to

the development of Danish design. The Asian collection is particularly strong – ranging from Japanese sword paraphernalia to Chinese Ming vases. Check out the selection in the museum shop (see p.64) if you fancy taking any pieces home with you.

The Danish Resistance

Despite pledging to remain neutral during World War II Denmark was occupied by German forces from April 9, 1940 until May 1945. While the occupation was not the bloodbath that unfurled elsewhere in Europe, **resistance groups** nonetheless sprung up, among them the "Churchill Club", a group of schoolboys who sabotaged German vehicles, and the Hvidsten Group (subject of a hit 2012 Danish film) who distributed British weapons from secret airdrops. One of the proudest moments of this period was the clandestine evacuation in October 1943 of the vast majority of Denmark's seven thousand Jews to safety in neutral Sweden; almost everyone seems to have an uncle or grandfather who was somehow involved.

Until recently the best place to get to grips with the Danish wartime experience was the **Frihedsmuseet** (Museum of Freedom, or Museum of Danish Resistance) at 7 Churchillparken. Sadly, on May 5, 2013, the museum was ravaged by fire – a tragedy attributed to arson. Fortunately, no archival records or artefacts – such as Himmler's eye patch, taken off him by the Allies as he was captured trying to flee in disguise – were lost in the blaze. At the time of press, construction of a new building was still in the design phase. In the meantime the Ryvangen Memorial Park in Hellerup commemorates resistance fighters executed by the Nazis.

KASTELLET

Daily 6am–10pm. MAP P.59, POCKET MAP G5

Surrounded by grassy ramparts and a series of moats, Copenhagen's quaint **Kastellet** (Citadel) is one of the best-preserved star-shaped fortresses in northern Europe. Brainchild of Christian IV and completed by Frederik III, it was constructed to defend the city from all sides, including from the city itself in case of rebellion. Its terraced rows of immaculate, mansard-roofed barracks, painted in warm red hues, are still occupied by troops, making this also one of Europe's oldest functioning military bases. The granite war memorial in its southwest corner, dedicated to the many Danish soldiers who have been lost in action around the world since 1948, was unveiled in 2011.

THE LITTLE MERMAID

MAP P.59, POCKET MAP G5

Sitting on a boulder in the Inner Harbour off the northern edge of Kastellet, looking forlornly out to sea, **The Little Mermaid** (*Den lille havfrue*) is the city's most famous symbol. The embodiment of Hans Christian Andersen's fairy-tale character, she was created by Danish sculptor Edvard Eriksen in 1913 and paid for by Carlsberg brewery magnate Carl Jakobsen. Considering her diminutive size and somewhat vacant facial expression, the cynical observer might find it difficult to fathom her appeal to the busloads of tourists that visit her 24 hours a day, though her tragic tale of doomed love for her dream prince still has a powerful hold on the Danish imagination. The statue has not had an easy life, either. She's been the frequent victim of radical groups, covered in paint several times and beheaded twice.

A more recent addition a few hundred metres to the north along the waterfront at Langeliniekaj, the Little Mermaid's iconoclastic "ugly sister" is far more entertaining. Part of Bjørn Nørgaard's sculpture garden **The Genetically Modified Paradise**, she sits like her older sister on a boulder in the water, but with body and limbs grotesquely elongated and contorted – perhaps a truer rendition of Andersen's Little Mermaid's suffering than the original statue.

THE LITTLE MERMAID

Shops

DESIGNMUSEUM DANMARK SHOP

Bredgade 68 ☎ 33 18 56 76, ⓦ design museum.dk. Tues & Thurs–Sun 11am–5pm, Wed 11am–9pm. MAP P.59, POCKET MAP G6

The Design Museum's shop is a great place for industrial design, and to pick up ceramics, glass, textiles and jewellery, all Danish-made. Check out Kaj Bojesen's wooden animal toys and the beautiful glassware by Holmegaard.

GALERIE ASBÆK

Bredgade 23 ☎ 33 15 40 04, ⓦ asbaek.dk. Tues–Fri 11am–6pm, Sat 11am–4pm. MAP P.59, POCKET MAP E11

This well-known art gallery sells works by some of the country's leading contemporary artists, including CoBrA painter Carl Henning-Pedersen (aka the "Scandinavian Chagall") and photographer Niels Bonde.

LØGISMOSE

Nordre Toldbod 16 ☎ 33 32 93 32, ⓦ loegismose.dk. Mon–Fri 10am–7pm, Sat 10am–5pm. MAP P.59, POCKET MAP G5

A cornucopia of fabulous wines and spirits is on sale at this deli on the Innerhavnen, as well as delicious cheeses and charcuterie from France, Spain and Italy. It's also an outlet for heavenly Summerbird chocolate (see p.76).

Cafés and restaurants

CAFÉ OSCAR

Bredgade 58 ☎ 33 12 50 10, ⓦ cafeoscar.dk. Daily 9.30am–11pm. MAP P.59, POCKET MAP G6

Upmarket corner café a short walk from Amalienborg, serving a selection of excellent smørrebrød (from 72kr), burgers, sandwiches and salads, plus a meat-focused evening menu. Fabulous food aside, it's to be seen hobnobbing with the rich and famous that most people come.

CAP HORN

Nyhavn 21 ☎ 33 12 85 04, ⓦ caphorn.dk. Daily 9am–midnight. MAP P.59, POCKET MAP E11

The best choice among the long row of overpriced restaurants along Nyhavns Kanal, *Cap Horn* serves largely organic fare, including juicy burgers (129kr) and always one or two seafood options (from 189kr).

EMMERYS

Store Strandstræde 21 ☎ 51 85 77 19, ⓦ emmerys.dk. Mon–Fri 7.30am–6pm, Sat & Sun 8am–5pm. MAP P.59, POCKET MAP E11

Part of an ever-expanding chain of café-bakeries, *Emmerys* is famous for its slow-risen organic bread, which you sample in sandwiches or as part of a breakfast platter. It's a great coffee stop, too, and treat yourself to a superb gooey brownie while you're at it.

CAP HORN

GRØNBECH & CHURCHILL

GEIST

Kongens Nytorv 8 ☎ 33 13 37 13,
ⓦ restaurantgeist.dk. Daily noon–1am.
MAP P.59, POCKET MAP E11

This hip but unpretentious
(and well-priced) spot is
presided over by ex-*Paustian*
chef Bo Bech. In the centre,
the open kitchen has stools
around it for diners'
observation, while the
thirty-dish menu focuses on
some inventive fusions such as
grilled octopus and
strawberries (165kr) or
vanilla ice cream, served
with olives, cinnamon and
liquorice (95kr).

GRØNBECH & CHURCHILL

Esplanaden 48 ☎ 32 21 32 30,
ⓦ gronbech-churchill.dk. Mon–Fri
noon–2.30pm & 6–10pm, Sat 6–10pm MAP
P.59, POCKET MAP G6

Located across from
Churchillparken, this rather
low-key Michelin-starred
restaurant is open for both
lunch and dinner. Choose
from the select and seasonal à
la carte list or put your
stomach in the hands of the
creative kitchen: the all-inclu-
sive, chef's choice "High
Roller" menu, which comes
with numerous servings, wine,
coffee and all the trimmings,
will set you back a cool

1874kr. A five-course lunch
menu of the chef's own
choosing is more humbly
priced at 500kr.

IDA DAVIDSEN

Store Kongensgade 70 ☎ 33 91 36 55,
ⓦ idadavidsen.dk. Mon–Fri 10.30am–5pm;
closed July. MAP P.59, POCKET MAP E10

When the craving strikes for
smørrebrød, it's to *Ida Davidsen*
that the Danish royals decamp
– and the elaborately assembled
smørrebrød (from 65kr) and
sandwiches are indeed fit for a
king. *Dyrlægens natmad*
(literally "vet's midnight snack"
– buttered rye bread smeared
with liver pâté and topped with
aspic and a slice of salted beef)
and the prawn sandwich are
particular highlights.

KAFFERIET

Esplanaden 44 ☎ 33 93 93 04, ⓦ kafferiet
.net. Mon–Fri 7.30am–6pm, Sat & Sun
10am–6pm. MAP P.59, POCKET MAP G6

Colourful and cosy little coffee
shop across from Kastellet with
a few tables inside and a couple
outside on the street, too.
There's delightful coffee and
home-made cakes, plus
interesting Italian confec-
tionery: sweets from Pastiglie
Leone and strong Amarelli
liquorice. A little gem in an
otherwise café-barren area.

MADKLUBBEN

Store Kongensgade 66 ☎ 33 32 32 34,
ⓦ madklubben.dk. Mon–Sat 5.30pm–
midnight. MAP P.59, POCKET MAP E10
Branch of the wildly popular
restaurant chain that offers
simple, tasty food with fast
and efficient service.

MASH

Bredgade 20 ☎ 33 13 93 00, ⓦ mashsteak
.dk. Lunch Mon–Fri noon–3pm; dinner
Mon–Wed & Sun 5.30–10pm; Thurs–Sat
5.30–11pm. MAP P.59, POCKET MAP F11
MASH stands for Modern
American Steak House, which
is exactly what you get – juicy
steaks in a US diner setting.
Starters (115kr) range from
snails with garlic to half a
grilled lobster and the steaks
(from 295kr) come in all
shapes and sizes – from
Uruguayan tenderloin to
American bone-in ribeye, via
(Aussie-sourced) Wagyu fillet.

MORMORS

Bredgade 45 ☎ 33 16 07 00, ⓦ mormors.dk.
Mon–Fri 8.30am–5pm, Sat 11.30am–5pm.
MAP P.59, POCKET MAP E10
A homely pit stop, *Mormors*
("Grandma's") easily lives up to
its name with its warm and
welcoming feel. There's hot
soup for the cold winter
months (55kr), a range of

freshly made juices (42kr),
sandwiches galore and a
counter full of delicious cakes.
Park yourself in one of the
window seats inside, or at the
pavement tables out front.

PAKHUSKÆLDEREN

Nyhavn 71 ☎ 33 43 62 14,
ⓦ pakhuskaelderen.com. Mon–Sat noon–
midnight. MAP P.59, POCKET MAP F11
Part of the grand *71 Nyhavn*
hotel overlooking Copenhagen's harbour, this stylish
gourmet restaurant features
plenty of exposed pine beams
and plenty of atmosphere.
Continental menu specialities
include *moules marinières*
(95kr) or breast of poularde
with basil and artichokes
(230kr). Also has a great bar
open all day.

REBEL

Store Kongensgade 52 ☎ 33 32 32 09,
ⓦ restaurantrebel.dk. Tues–Sat 5.30pm–
midnight. MAP P.59, POCKET MAP E10
Compact restaurant spread
over two floors serving elegant
French-inspired tapas. It's
especially renowned for its beef
tartare, served with rhubarb,
herbed mayonnaise and
vinaigrette, and turbot served
with escargot, lobster glaze and
tarragon. Four small dishes
400kr.

SALT

Toldbodgade 24 ☎ 33 74 14 44,
ⓦ saltrestaurant.dk. Daily noon to 4pm &
5–10.30pm. MAP P.59, POCKET MAP F11

Hotel Admiral's characterful
restaurant has seating both in
the charming wood-beamed
interior and out on the
waterfront. The excellent
seafood menu (from 395kr)
and the mouthwatering
selection of Nordic cheeses
(135kr) can hardly be bettered.

TASTE

Store Kongensgade 80–82 ☎ 33 93 77 97,
ⓦ tastedeli.eu. Mon–Fri 9.30am–6pm, Sat &
Sun 10am–6pm. MAP P.59, POCKET MAP E10

This fabulous deli (with a few
tables out front) serves gorgeous
home-made salads, sandwiches
plus a range of exquisite cakes
– though as everything is of tip
top quality nothing comes
cheap. Try the grilled goat's
cheese, beetroot and walnut
sandwich, with a honey and
rosemary dressing (78kr).

VESPA

Store Kongensgade 90 ☎ 33 11 37 00,
ⓦ cofoco.dk. Mon–Sat 5.30pm–midnight.
MAP P.59, POCKET MAP F6

Part of the Cofoco "food
empire", which follows a simple
no-frills concept. What's on
offer is a well-prepared
four-course Italian set menu for
275kr. Restrictive perhaps, but
excellent value for money.

Bars

DEN VANDRETTE

Havnegade 53A ☎ 72 14 82 28,
ⓦ denvandrette.dk. Tues–Sat 5–11pm. MAP
P.59, POCKET MAP F12

Wine cellar next to Copenhagen's newest harbour bridge,
with a bare decor of brick and
oak, soft lighting and a range of
lesser-known biodynamic and
organic wines behind the
counter.

TOLDBODEN

Nordre Toldbod 24 ☎ 33 93 07 60,
ⓦ toldboden.com. May–Sept Mon–Thurs &
Sun 10am–10pm, Fri & Sat 10am–2am. MAP
P.59, POCKET MAP G5

With great views of the Inner
Harbour, *Toldboden* has few
rivals for the title of Copenhagen's most stunningly located
bar. It's a great place for drinks
during the week, particularly in
summer when you can chill out
in the deckchairs. As well as its
bar/ clubbing profile, *Toldboden*
also offers a popular weekend
brunch and grill buffet.

Club

SUNDAY

Lille Kongensgade 16 ⓦ sundayclub.dk.
Fri–Sat 11.30pm–5am. MAP P.59, POCKET MAP D11

Much-hyped nightclub
frequented by local celebs and
wannabes, the latest incarnation of the promoters behind
now-defunct Simons. To
further the mystique, a
scrambler jams up clubbers'
mobile phones once inside.

VESPA

Rosenborg and around

Christian IV's Renaissance summer palace, the Rosenborg Slot, provides a regal contrast with the crowded streets of the inner city to the east. To its west, running from Østerport station in the north to Vesterport in the south is an almost continuous string of attractive parks and gardens. Apart from being lovely places to explore, they also house a couple of significant art museums: the Statens Museum for Kunst and Hirschsprungske Samling, and the city's Botanical Gardens. It was thanks to visionary Town Planner Ferdinand Mekdahl that the ring of ramparts and bastions encircling the city here were maintained as a green belt in 1857. The area between the ramparts and the lake later developed into sought-after residential areas and streets such as Nansensgade have a strong neighbourhood feel.

ROSENBORG SLOT

4A Østervoldgade ☎ 33 15 32 86,
Ⓦ rosenborgslot.dk. Castle: May, Sept & Oct daily 10am–4pm; June–Aug daily 10am–5pm; Nov–April Tues–Sun 10am–2pm. 90kr, 130kr for combined ticket with Amalienborg.
Gardens: sunrise to sunset; free.
MAP PP70–71, POCKET MAP E6

A Disney-esque fairy-tale palace, the **Rosenborg Slot** was originally built as a summer residence for Christian IV, a retreat from the rabble at Christiansborg. Completed in 1634, it's a grand red-brick Renaissance edifice decorated with spires and towers and ornate Dutch gables. The palace remained a royal residence until 1838, when it was opened to the public.

The star exhibit inside is the **crown jewels**, chief among them the Crown of the Absolute Monarch which weighs in at a

Park life

Based around the Rosenborg Slot, the beautifully manicured **Kongens Have** (King's Garden) is Copenhagen's oldest park and a favoured spot in summer when there is live music and performances in the puppet theatre (June–Aug daily except Mon 2 & 3pm; free; ⓦmarionetteatret.dk). Stretching north from the Botanisk Have (Botanical Gardens), the undulating hills of **Østre Anlæg** are part of the old fortifications and house a number of different children's playgrounds including one in front of the National Museum of Art. **Ørstedsparken**, with its rolling hills and rampart lake, is a popular place to go in winter for skating and downhill sledging. There are also two innovative playgrounds here, one with staff at hand to show you the ropes. Come nightfall it becomes a gay hangout (in case you were wondering about the signs promoting safe sex).

hefty two kilos and sports two massive sapphires. The jewels are kept locked in the basement Treasury, behind thick steel doors. Also downstairs are the priceless wines of the Royal cellar, only cracked open at very special occasions. Before heading down here it's worth taking in Frederik III's lavish marble room with its extravagant stucco ceiling and a chess set made up of Danish and Swedish pieces (in reference to the war he lost to Karl Gustav in 1658). Another highlight of the palace is the magnificent **Long Hall** on the second floor with its gilded coronation throne, made from narwhal tusk, and three silver lions standing guard.

BOTANISK HAVE

Gothersgade 128 ⓦ botanik.snm.ku.dk. Daily: May–Sept 8.30am–6pm; Oct–April 8.30am–4pm. MAP PP.70–71, POCKET MAP E6

Relocated in 1874 from a small park behind Charlottenborg palace (p.60) the **Botanisk Have** (Botanical Gardens)

packs in pretty much every plant you'll find in Denmark together with several exotic species. It's a pleasant and peaceful place to wander, with its long squiggly pond clearly showing the area's previous incarnation as the city ramparts. Among the many greenhouses in the gardens, the grand Palm House overshadows them all. It was donated by brewing magnate Carl Jacobsen who was deeply involved in its design and various ingenious temperature and humidity controls. You will also find houses for cacti, orchids, alpine plants, and a new greenhouse for endangered species (check the website for their specific opening times).

The Botanical Museum, part of the gardens, is currently closed. A brand new National Natural History Museum, complete with innovative underground architecture, is due to open in 2020 at the northern end of the gardens.

Rosenborg and around

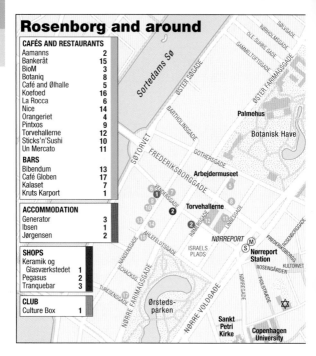

CAFÉS AND RESTAURANTS

Aamanns	2
Bankeråt	15
BioM	3
Botaniq	8
Café and Ølhalle	5
Koefoed	16
La Rocca	6
Nice	14
Orangeriet	4
Pintxos	9
Torvehallerne	12
Sticks'n'Sushi	10
Un Mercato	11

BARS

Bibendum	13
Café Globen	17
Kalaset	7
Kruts Karport	1

ACCOMMODATION

Generator	3
Ibsen	1
Jørgensen	2

SHOPS

Keramik og Glasværkstedet	1
Pegasus	2
Tranquebar	3

CLUB

Culture Box	1

STATENS MUSEUM FOR KUNST

Sølvgade 48–50 ☏ 33 74 84 94, ⓦ smk.dk.
Tues & Thurs–Sun 10am–5pm, Wed
10am–8pm. Permanent exhibitions &
X-rummet free, charge for changing exhibits
MAP ABOVE, POCKET MAP E5

Found in the southeastern
corner of Østre Anlæg park, the
vast **Statens Museum for Kunst**
(National Museum of Art)

houses the bulk of Christian II's
extensive collection of
European paintings and
sculptures. Housed in an 1896
building by Dahlerup (see also
Ny Carlsberg Glyptotek, p.34)
and complemented by a
modern extension in 1998, the
collection is divided into
European art from the
fourteenth to the eighteenth
century, Danish and Nordic Art
from 1750 to 1900, French art
from 1900–1930, and modern
art from the twentieth century.
Trying to see it all in one day is
almost impossible. Instead, if
you're interested in Danish art,
head straight for the second
floor where works from the
so-called Golden Age – the
nineteenth century – are
displayed in largely chrono-
logical order. Look out
especially for the beautifully lit
paintings of the Skagen school

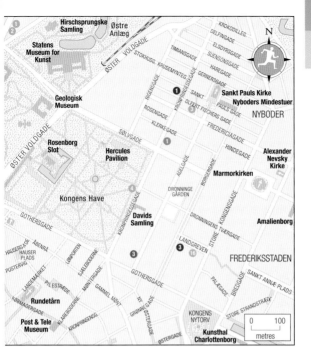

– among them P.S. Krøyer and Anna Ancher. Look out too for the stark almost photographic scenes of Copenhagen in the nineteenth century by Vilhelm Hammershøi. On the second floor you'll also find work from the twentieth-century CoBrA movement (a collection of artists from Copenhagen, Brussels and Amsterdam). Contemporary international art is displayed in the museum's new extension. Recent temporary exhibits have included Matisse and Miró.

HIRSCHSPRUNGSKE SAMLING

Stockholmsgade 20 ☎35 42 03 36, ⓦhirschsprung.dk. Tues–Sun 11am–4pm. 90kr, free some Weds. MAP ABOVE, POCKET MAP F5

More manageable than the Statens Museum, the **Hirschsprung Collection** focuses on art from the Danish Golden Age (1800–1850), donated by Heinrich Hirschsprung, a second-generation German Jew who had made his fortune in tobacco. Housed in a beautiful Neoclassical pavilion, paintings are displayed in small intimate rooms (a condition Hirschsprung set before handing over his collection to the state). As at the Staten Museum, the work of the Skagen artists P.S. Krøyer and Anna Ancher particularly stands out. Tranquil bucolic landscapes by P.C. Skovgaard and Johan Lundbye are also worth noting. More entertaining are the gossip-magazine-like paintings by Kristian Zahrt-mann who depicted eighteenth-century royal scandals such as English-born Queen Caroline Mathilde's affair with court physician Johann Friedrich Struensee.

ARBEJDERMUSEET

Rømersgade 22 ☎ 33 93 25 75. ⓦ arbejdermuseet.dk. Daily 10am–4pm, 65kr. MAP PP.70–71, POCKET MAP A18

Dedicated to the Danish workers movement, **Arbejdermuseet** is housed in the group's old meeting house from 1878 and covers the cultural history of the Danish working class from 1850 onwards. Although it's probably more of interest to Danes, the historic assembly hall is worth a peek. Its tranquil bucolic decor witnessed some of the movement's most significant gatherings, not least the Socialist World Congress of 1910 which had Lenin himself in attendance (there's a Russian-made statue of him in the foyer dating from the late 1980s). The children's section, although mostly in Danish, is also popular, and often noisy, featuring doll's houses, dressing-up gear, colouring-in books and even a small pretend brewery. There's also a museum shop selling iconic workers' posters from the old Soviet Union and a basement restaurant (p.75) knocking out traditional workers' dishes from the last century.

DAVIDS SAMLING

Kronprinsessegade 30 ☎ 33 73 49 49. ⓦ davidmus.dk. Tues & Thurs–Sun 10am–5pm, Wed 10am–9pm. Free. MAP PP.70–71, POCKET MAP B18

Spread over all five floors of an eighteenth-century apartment building, the captivating **Davids Samling** comprises the remarkable collection of one C.L. David (1878–1960), a Danish lawyer who devoted

Dining with the Danes

Danish food exploded on the global stage in 2010, when *Noma* was named the world's top restaurant. Since then, simple Nordic dishes made from seasonal, locally sourced ingredients (preferably foraged from nearby) have taken Copenhagen by storm. While *Noma*'s time at the top has been put on pause – it's expected to close at the end of 2016 before being transformed into an urban farm (see p.80) – the Danish capital continues to garner more Michelin stars than Stockholm, Oslo and Helsinki put together, and boasts a slew of eateries headed by *Noma* protégés, such as *Relæ* (p.103) and *Amass* (p.83), where the Nordic kitchen can be sampled while still leaving your bank balance intact. Alternatively head straight to Copenhagen Street Food (p.84) or to the Torvehallerne food market (p.76) to shop where the chefs shop.

Since its opening in 2011, the new **Torvehallerne** food market (see p.76) has been a resounding success, attracting over sixty thousand visitors a week to its artisan stalls and restaurants. **Israels Plads** square next door, traditionally known for its flower stalls, has finally reopened after two years of renovation, and this busy square fills with people in the summer, where its "flying carpet" architecture merges with neighbouring Ørsted-sparken. The square was given its current name in 1968 in memory of Jewish persecution in Denmark during World War II.

his life to the acquisition of fine and applied art. It's a labyrinth of rooms, and the museum plan handed out on arrival will prove essential. The highlight without doubt is the extensive exhibition of Islamic art on the third and fourth floors. One of the most important in the West, it includes delicate Persian miniatures, striking blue Ottoman mosaics and beautifully decorated glass bowls from Egypt and Syria. David's collections of eighteenth- and nineteenth-century porcelain and furniture and twentieth-century art (look out for the evocative landscape paintings by Vilhelm Hammershøi and the extravagant French ceramics) are also impressive but don't match the heights of the Islamic finds.

TORVEHALLERNE AND ISRAELS PLADS

Market halls: Frederiksborggade 21 ⓦ torvehallernekbh.dk. Mon–Thurs 10am–7pm, Fri 10am–8pm, Sat 10am–6pm, Sun 11am–5pm. MAP PP.70-71, POCKET MAP B10

NYBODER

Nyboder Mindestuer, 24 Sankt Paulsgade ☎ 50 56 49 69, ⓦ nybodersmindestuer.dk. Sun 11am–2pm. 20kr. MAP PP.70-71, POCKET MAP F6.

Standing out in contrast to the area's grand regal mansions, the colourful and quaint **Nyboder** district is made up of a series of rows of cute, predominantly ochre-coloured terraced houses. The area was originally built in the 1630s to provide housing for Christian IV's ever-expanding naval fleet, though most of the current buildings date from the eighteenth century – all except for a single row of houses along Sankt Paulsgade, where the **Nyboders Mindestuer** (Nyboder Memorial Rooms) has been largely kept intact and functions as a museum. Diminutive though Nyboder's houses may be, this has always been a sought-after place to live, with its own private school and hospital, and demand remains high, particularly since (as of 2006) priority is no longer given to military personnel.

Shops

KERAMIK OG GLASVÆRKSTEDET

Kronprinsessegade 43 ☎ 33 32 89 91,
ⓦ keramikogglasvaerkstedet.dk. Wed–Fri
noon to 6pm, Sat 11am–2pm. MAP PP.70–71,
POCKET MAP F6

Funky workshop-cum-gallery
selling delicate and minimalist
ceramics and glassware made
on the premises by four
independent artists.

PEGASUS

Nørre Farimagsgade 53 ☎ 33 32 56 50,
ⓦ pegasus.dk. Mon & Thurs 3.30–6.30pm.
MAP PP.70–71, POCKET MAP A10

Nerdy basement store selling a
huge selection of comics and
graphic novels (new and
secondhand) from around the
globe with an especially good
selection of American comics.

TRANQUEBAR

Borgergade 14 ☎ 33 12 55 12, ⓦ tranquebar
.net. Mon–Fri 10am–6pm, Sat 10am–4pm. MAP
PP.70–71, POCKET MAP E10

Well-stocked book and music
shop with a vast selection of
travel literature and world music
(and, of course, a good range of
Rough Guides). The bookstore
café sells lunch platters
(noon–3pm) from *Koefoed* (see
opposite), up the road.

Cafés and restaurants

AAMANNS

Øster Farimagsgade 10 ☎ 35 55 33 44,
ⓦ aamanns.dk. Restaurant: Wed–Sat noon to
4pm & 6–11pm, Sun noon–4pm; takeaway:
Mon–Fri 10.30am–8pm, Sat 11am–4.30pm,
Sun noon–4.30pm. MAP PP.70–71, POCKET MAP E5

This stylish ode to traditional
Danish open sandwiches makes
hands-down the city's best
smørrebrød. Head chef Adam

AAMANNS

Aamanns ensures everything is
free range and sourced from
local Danish farmers
(four-course menu 345kr). It's
perfect for a visit with children,
too, who love the bite-sized
portions. You can either eat in
or take away in smart little
picnic-friendly boxes.

BANKERÅT

Ahlefeldtsgade 27–29 ☎ 33 93 69 88,
ⓦ bankeraat.dk. Mon–Fri 9.30am to midnight,
Sat & Sun 10.30am to midnight. MAP PP.70–71,
POCKET MAP A10

Oldie but goodie Nansensgade
café which is just as popular
now as when it opened in the
80s with its largely unchanged
quirky decor. Its signature
breakfast/brunch Morgenkom-
plex comes in lots of different
variations including "Full
Engelsk". Turns into a popular
bar come evening.

BIOM

Fredericiagade 78 ☎ 33 32 24 66, ⓦ biom.dk.
Tues–Sat 11.30am–11pm; Brunch Sat & Sun
10am–2pm. MAP PP.70–71, POCKET MAP F6

Cool organic restaurant
offering a good range of
vegetarian options and a few

tasty meaty ones, too. If in doubt try the lunchtime mushroom risotto (99kr).

BOTANIQ

Frederiksborggade 26 ☎ 33 36 33 30, ⓦ botaniq.com. Mon–Sat 11.30am–9pm. MAP PP.70–71, POCKET MAP B10

Priding itself on a green sustainable menu, *Botaniq* makes wonderful vegetarian, vegan and raw combos such as spelt risotto served with quinoa, capers, cream and mushrooms (115kr). They also serve excellent smoothies and organic cocktails and wines.

CAFE AND ØLHALLE

Rømersgade 22 ⓦ arbejdermuseet.dk. Jan–Oct Mon–Sat 11am–5pm, Nov & Dec Mon–Sun 11am–5pm. MAP PP.70–71, POCKET MAP B10

You may find the traditional nineteenth-century worker's fare served here a little heavy, but it is authentic and very tasty. Try the *Dagens Husmandsret* (daily special) for 99kr, or the *Bondekonens stegte sild* (farmer's wife's fried herring) for 78kr. Also on the menu are some old-school desserts.

LA ROCCA

KOEFOED

Landgreven 3 ☎ 56 48 22 24, ⓦ restaurant-koefoed.dk. Tues–Sat noon–3pm & 5.30–9.30pm. MAP PP.70–71, POCKET MAP E10

Elegant *Koefoed* is an ode to the gourmet island of Bornholm, famous for its slow-food ethos and quality produce. The lunchtime smørrebrød (from 95kr) has won awards, while the dinner menu starts at 220kr for a main (Bornholmer rooster or cod with oysters, for example). Eat in the atmospheric, vaulted, stone-walled interior or outside on streetside tables.

LA ROCCA

Vendersgade 23–25 ☎ 33 12 66 55, ⓦ larocca.dk. Daily noon–10.30pm. MAP PP.70–71, POCKET MAP A10

Classical Italian restaurant at *Ibsens Hotel*, offering refined Italian dining such as a fine mixed seafood grill (245kr) and a couple of good pizzas, too.

NICE

Nansensgade 66 ☎ 33 12 10 22, ⓦ cafenice .dk. Mon–Thurs & Sun 11am–11pm, Fri & Sat 10am to midnight. MAP PP.70–71, POCKET MAP A10

Small, ramshackle basement café-restaurant seemingly transplanted from Paris, producing outstanding steak (179kr) and *moules frites* (150kr).

ORANGERIET

Kronprinsessegade 13 ☎ 33 11 13 07, ⓦ restaurant-orangeriet.dk. Mon–Sat 11.30am–3pm & 6–10pm. MAP PP.70–71, POCKET MAP D10

Atmospheric glass-encased café-restaurant located along the western wall of Kongens Have, with great views of the gardens, serving excellent smørrebrød for lunch and more substantial meals for dinner starting at 195kr for grilled skate with cauliflower purée.

A taste of Torvehallerne

A few of Torvehallerne's best stalls are listed below and should be visited in their own right:

Unika (stall F5) – retail outlet for cheeses usually only sold to Michelin-starred restaurants.

Grød (stall A8) – sells porridge, risotto and anything else eaten with a spoon, exclusively.

The Coffee Collective (stall C1) – the best coffee in town.

Hallernes Smørrebrød (stall F2)

– great smørrebrød selected from a large display cabinet; Mikkeller on draught.

Gorms Pizza (stall G1) – freshly made pizza from a wood-fired oven.

Tapa del Torro (stall F10) – delicious home-made tapas.

Summerbird (stall A3) – chocolate made in heaven.

TORVEHALLERNE

PINTXOS

Nansensgade 63 ☎ 33 93 66 55, ⓦ pintxostapas.dk. Daily 5–11pm. MAP PP.70–71, POCKET MAP A10

Genuine Spanish restaurant with genuine Spanish waiters, and tapas galore (from 49kr) in a romantic courtyard.

TORVEHALLERNE

Frederiksborggade 21 ⓦ torvehallernekbh.dk. Mon–Thurs 10am–7pm, Fri 10am–8pm, Sat 10am–6pm, Sun 11am–5pm. Coffee and freshly baked bread available Mon–Sat from 8am, Sun from 9am. Restaurants and takeaways stay open an hour later than the market. MAP PP.70–71, POCKET MAP B10

Denmark's biggest and best food market. It's split into two long open-sided halls, one featuring meat, cheese and fish and a non-smelly section where you'll find chocolate, bread and the

like. In between are plenty of outdoor benches at which to eat. A great way to explore Torvehallerne is to join the city's new Food Tours (box, p.131).

STICKS'N'SUSHI

Nansensgade 59 ☎ 33 11 14 07, ⓦ sushi.dk. Mon–Thurs & Sun 10am–10.30pm, Fri & Sat 10am–11pm. MAP PP.70–71, POCKET MAP A10

Copenhagen's original purveyors of raw fish to the masses. Starting out some twenty years ago, they now have branches across the city (and in London). They can still make a mean sushi and also specialize in yakitori sticks (marinated skewers of meat and fish) as well as an outstanding array of salads, best of which is the scrumptious fish-bowl salad (149kr).

UN MERCATO

Torvehallerne, Frederiksborggade 21.
Mon–Sat 11.30am–11pm, Sun 11.30am–
10pm. MAP PP.70–71, POCKET MAP B10

No-nonsense Italian rotisserie
on the first floor of Torvehallerne, run by the people
behind *Cofoco* restaurants.
The lunchtime flame-grilled
chicken or porchetta
sandwiches (65kr) are
mouthwatering – even just
writing about them.

Bars

BIBENDUM

Nansensgade 45 ☎ 33 33 07 74, ⓦ bibendum
.dk. Mon–Sat 4pm–midnight. MAP PP.70–71,
POCKET MAP A10

Small cosy basement wine bar
with a huge selection of wine,
all of which are sold by
the glass as well as by the
bottle. Also good nibbles
(from 85kr) to soak up the
alcohol such as cheese and
charcuterie platters and a
delicious fish soup.

CAFÉ GLOBEN

Turesensgade 2b ☎ 33 93 00 77,
ⓦ cafegloben.dk. Mon–Thurs 5–10pm, Fri
5pm–1am. MAP PP.70–71, POCKET MAP A11

Laidback travellers' haunt
halfway between a club and a
café with lots of guidebooks
lying around and people keen
to talk about their latest
adventures. Selling a good
range of brews from home and
abroad, they don't mind if you
bring your own food and eat at
their tables.

KALASET

Vendersgade 16 ☎ 33 33 00 35. Mon–Thurs
10am–midnight, Fri & Sat 10am–2am, Sun
10am–11pm. MAP PP.70–71, POCKET MAP A10

Quirky shabby-chic basement
café which spills out onto the
pavement during summer when
it's an excellent spot to enjoy
the sunshine while sipping a
cool drink. During weekends a
DJ gets the party going.

KRUTS KARPORT

Øster Farimagsgade 12 ☎ 35 26 86 38.
Mon–Thurs 2pm–midnight, Fri & Sat
2pm–2am, Sun 2–9pm. MAP PP.70–71,
POCKET MAP E5

Copenhagen's first French-style
café, *Kruts Karport* stocks the
city's largest selection of
whisky, and is one of the few
places you can order an
absinthe. That said, the
selection of foreign draught
beer is not bad either.

Club

CULTURE BOX

Kronprinsessegade 54 ☎ 33 32 50 50,
ⓦ culture-box.dk. Fri & Sat 11pm–6am. MAP
PP.70–71, POCKET MAP F6

Spread over two floors, with a
Berlin-style industrial decor,
this popular bar-club keeps
going until the wee hours of
the morning. Revellers tend to
get the party started first at
The White Box cocktail bar
next door.

BIBENDUM

Christianshavn and Holmen

With its tight network of narrow canals and cobbled streets, Christianshavn – sometimes known as Little Amsterdam – is one of the city's most charming areas. Water is omnipresent, perhaps not surprising given that the island was constructed from reclaimed land in the sixteenth century to form a defensive arc around the city. For the most part the attractions here are low-key, though Christianshavn's principal source of tourist intrigue – the unique "Freetown" of Christiania, home to one of the world's most famous alternative communities – pulls in almost a million visitors a year. To the north, former naval base Holmen and its neighbouring islands have been re-energized after decades of disuse with post-industrial developments like the national opera house and an old shipyard, B&W Hallerne, that was rebuilt to host 2014's Eurovision Song Contest. To the south, Islands Brygge quay stretches along the harbourfront of Amager, and is worth visiting for its waterside park and lively cultural centre.

CHRISTIANSHAVNS KANAL

MAP OPPOSITE, POCKET MAP E14–F14

Lined on both sides by cobbled streets and colourful merchant's houses, the tranquil **Christian-shavns Kanal** originally provided the main way of accessing the island. This picturesque area is redolent of old Amsterdam, and indeed was designed by a Dutch architect, Johan Semp, who was commissioned in the early seventeenth century by Christian IV to plan the district.

Then as now, Christian-shavn's main square, **Christianshavn Torv**, was the focal point of public transport to the island – today there's a metro station (underground) and constant flow of buses, as well as a canal-boat stop. A notable exception to the imposing historic buildings around the square is the

modernist **Lagkagehuset** (Layercake House) at Torvegade 45. It created riotous debate when it was built in 1931 as it was felt it didn't blend in to its historic surroundings but today is deemed a national treasure.

CHRISTIANSHAVNS KANAL

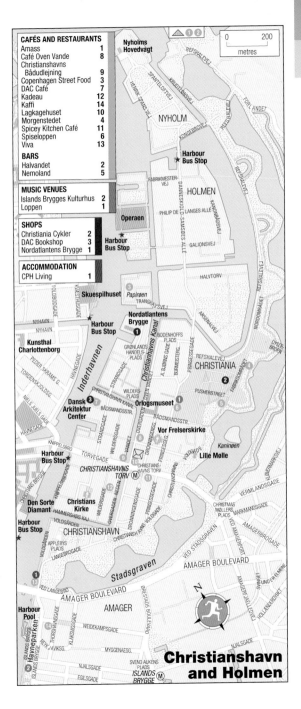

CAFÉS AND RESTAURANTS

Amass	1
Café Oven Vande	8
Christianshavns Bådudlejning	9
Copenhagen Street Food	3
DAC Café	7
Kadeau	12
Kaffi	14
Lagkagehuset	10
Morgenstedet	4
Spicey Kitchen Café	11
Spiseloppen	6
Viva	13

BARS

Halvandet	2
Nemoland	5

MUSIC VENUES

Islands Brygges Kulturhus	2
Loppen	1

SHOPS

Christiania Cykler	2
DAC Bookshop	3
Nordatlantens Brygge	1

ACCOMMODATION

CPH Living	1

Christianshavn and Holmen

CHRISTIANS KIRKE

Strandgade 1 ⓦ christianskirke.dk.
Tues–Fri 10am–4pm. MAP P.79, POCKET MAP E14

Surrounded by modern offices
and apartments, Eigtved's
Rococo **Christians Kirke** (1759)
looks oddly out of place. It was
originally built for the city's
German congregation and still
functions as a church, though its
theatre-like interior makes it an
excellent music venue.

ORLOGSMUSEET

Overgaden Oven Vandet 58 ⓣ 41 20 63 74.
ⓦ natmus.dk, Tues–Sun noon–4pm.
MAP P.79, POCKET MAP F13

Part of the National Museum
(see p.36), **The Royal Danish
Naval Museum** is housed in an
old naval hospital overlooking
the canal. Wander among
incredibly detailed, to-scale ship
models from sixteenth-century
galleons to modern submarines;
there is also a model ship that
children can play on.

VOR FRELSERSKIRKE

Skt Annæ Gade 29 ⓣ 32 54 68 83, ⓦ www
.vorfrelserskirke.dk. Church: daily
11am–3.30pm; free. Tower: June to mid-Sept
daily 10am–7pm; mid-Sept to May daily
10am–4pm (Sun opens at 10.30am); 35kr.
MAP P.79, POCKET MAP F13

Capped by an iconic church
tower, its soaring spire wrapped
in a gilded spiral external
staircase which culminates in a
globe carrying a flag-waving
Jesus, **Vor Frelserskirke** (Our
Saviour's Church) is an
unmissable feature of the
Christianshavn skyline.
Constructed in the late 1600s,
the church owes its opulence to
Christian V, whose status as
Denmark's first absolute
monarch is underlined by some
lavish Baroque flourishes.
Inside, look out especially for
the two stucco elephants
holding up the gigantic
three-storey organ, though the
real highlight is the ascent of the
tower, accessed by a separate
entrance. There are 400 steps to
the top, 150 of which are
external – quite a challenge on a
busy summer's day – but the
stupendous views across the city
are ample reward.

CHRISTIANIA

Main entrance on Prinsessegade.
Infocaféen daily noon–6pm. Guided tours
(starting at the main entrance) Sat & Sun
3pm; 40kr. MAP P.79, POCKET MAP G8

A self-proclaimed autonomous
enclave with its own governance

Christiania: reinventing itself to survive

Ever since its inception more than forty years ago, residents have struggled
to defend Christiania's existence. Frequent clashes over the residents'
occupation (for free) of prime city real estate, past non-payment of taxes,
with police over the drug trade and finally, the government's plans for
redevelopment, forced temporary closure in 2011. Residents managed to broker
a remarkable deal with the government, however, to buy back the buildings at
sub-market rates (still a cool 76 million kroner), and to pay annual rent of 6
million kroner for the rest, issuing so-called People's Shares
(ⓦ christianiafolkeaktie.dk) as a way for outside supporters to fund its survival.
Now, the community may have a surprising ally in the form of Rene Redzepi,
whose plans to rebuild world-acclaimed restaurant *Noma* on a scrappy plot of
ground next to Christiania, with urban gardens to source much of the
restaurant's produce (expected opening date 2017) has been described as a
stroke of "insane genius".

MURAL, CHRISTIANIA

and rules, **Freetown Christiania** is Copenhagen's main alternative claim to fame. Ever since 1971, when a group of homeless Copenhageners first occupied the disused Bådsmandsstræde army barracks, Christiania has attracted controversy, its very existence perennially threatened (see box, opposite). Today, thanks in no small part to its open cannabis trade, it's one of the city's most visited tourist attractions. Despite its dishevelled look and whacked-out feel, it's a remarkable place. Egalitarian, creative and ecologically minded, the ideals of its thousand-or-so residents have resulted in some truly unique self-built homes, imaginative businesses, and a host of artistic venues.

Extending for around 1km along the bastions that straddle Christian IV's picturesque defensive moat, there is quite a lot of Christiania to see, and the best way to experience it is either to join one of the immensely informative (if inevitably one-sided) guided tours, or buy a copy of the *Christiania Guide* (20kr) from the Infocaféen, in the **Loppebygningen** building to the left of the main entrance. Housed within the same

building, a former artillery magazine, are the **Gallopperiet** art gallery (🐨gallopperiet.dk), *Spiseloppen* restaurant (see p.85) and Loppen music venue (see p.85).

Continuing along the main artery, you reach **Carl Madsens Plads**, lined with stalls selling knick-knacks and fast food, which marks the beginning of **Pusherstreet** – impossible to miss from its unmistakeable aroma. Lining the street are rows of well-stocked shacks selling everything from pre-rolled joints to smoking paraphernalia. A couple of basic rules apply on Pusher-street: don't run (or the stallholders will think there's a police raid) and don't take photos. Also remember that the use of hash is still a criminal offence in Denmark.

Following the edge of the moat around from *Nemoland* (see p.85) leads you into the quieter, greener and more residential area. Here you will find some of Christiania's most ingenious alternative dwellings. A pedestrian bridge crosses the moat at the next bastion, or you can continue along past four bastions to the public road at the end, and follow the moat path back on the opposite side.

DANSK ARKITEKTUR CENTER

Strandgade 27B ☎ 32 57 19 30, ⓦ dac.dk. Mon–Fri 10am–5pm, Wed until 9pm, Sat & Sun 10am–5pm. Exhibition 40kr. Architectural tours May–Sept Sun 2pm; 125kr; bike rental not included. MAP P.79, POCKET MAP F13

Housed in a beautifully restored warehouse building on the waterfront next to the former naval dry dock (the most advanced of its kind when constructed in the sixteenth century), the **Danish Architecture Centre** hosts changing exhibitions of new Danish and international architecture, has a well-stocked bookshop (see opposite), and a first-floor café with perhaps the best views in town (see p.84). In summer the centre organizes weekly **tours** on foot or by bike to an area of Copenhagen of particular interest to fans of new architecture – typically to Ørestaden, Holmen or along the harbourfront (tours usually start at the tourist information office on Vesterbrogade; book on ⓦ dac.dk).

OPERAEN

Holmen ☎ 33 69 69 69, ⓦ operaen.dk. Tours most Sat & Sun; 100kr. Harbour Bus. MAP P.79, POCKET MAP G6

Occupying a prominent position on the compact island of Holmen diametrically across the water from the Marmorkirken, the Henning Larsen-designed **Operaen** (Opera House) is visible from almost any point along the harbour. It's a striking building, surmounted by an enormous flat roof that delicately overhangs the water's edge, while the no-expense-spared interior features gigantic outlandish lighting globes, designed by Danish-Icelandic artist Oluf Eliasson, in the foyer; note too the Jura sandstone walls inset with

OPERAEN

masses of tiny fossils. To gain access, though, you'll need either to see a performance (doors open 2hr beforehand) or join a guided tour.

ISLANDS BRYGGE

MAP P.79, POCKET MAP F9

Just south of Christianshavn, on the island of Amager, the Islands Brygge development is fast becoming one of the city's most happening areas. Much of this former industrial harbour strip has been converted into a waterfront park, the **Havneparken** – popular with people from all walks of life, from parents with prams to parkour enthusiasts – with cultural activity focused around the Islands Brygges Kulturhus (see p.85). Best of all, however, is the innovative, council-run **harbour pool** (June–Aug Mon–Fri 7am–7pm, Sat & Sun 9am–7pm; free), the perfect place to cool off in the summer.

The quayside walkway extends all the way south to the bicycle and pedestrian bridge, officially the **Bryggebroen** ("Quay bridge"), which gives access to Fisketorvet and Vesterbro.

Shops

CHRISTIANIA CYKLER

Mælkeven 83A, Christiania ☎ 32 54 87 48, Ⓦ christianiabikes.dk. Mon–Fri 9am–5pm, Sat 11am–3pm. MAP P.79, POCKET MAP G8

Classic, sturdy and super-cool, Christiania Bikes' hand-crafted three-wheel cargo cycles are one of the city's icons. Prices start at 10,100kr.

DAC BOOKSHOP

Strandgade 27B ☎ 32 57 19 30, Ⓦ dac-bookshop.dk. Mon–Fri 8am–6pm, Wed till 9pm, Sat & Sun 10am–5pm. MAP P.79, POCKET MAP F13

The Danish Architecture Centre's attractive bookshop stocks just about every title on modern architecture you could ever wish for.

NORDATLANTENS BRYGGE

Strandgade 91 ☎ 32 83 37 00, Ⓦ bryggen.dk. Mon–Fri 10am–5pm, Sat & Sun noon–5pm. Entry (also for shop) 40kr. MAP P.79, POCKET MAP G7

Housed in an enormous eighteenth-century warehouse, Nordatlantens Brygge promotes artistic and cultural links between Denmark, Greenland, Iceland and the Faroe Islands. A small store at the back sells regional music and crafts such as Icelandic knitwear and sealskin slippers from Greenland.

Cafés and restaurants

AMASS

Refshalevej 153 ☎ 43 58 43 30, Ⓦ amassrestaurant.com. Tues–Thurs 6pm–midnight; Fri & Sat noon–3.30pm & 6pm–midnight. MAP P79, POCKET MAP H5

Amass' opening on industrial Refshaleøen island in 2013 created quite a stir: owner and head chef, Matthew Orlando is formerly of *Noma*, and *Amass* is similarly focused on local produce but dining is simpler here, with a "drop-in" table and communal eating encouraged.

CAFÉ OVEN VANDE

Overgaden Oven Vandet 44 ☎ 32 95 96 02, Ⓦ cafeovenvande.dk. Daily 10am–midnight. MAP P.79, POCKET MAP F13

With tables and chairs spilling out onto the pavement, this Christianshavn institution is a fine place to enjoy an excellent lunchtime smørrebrød platter (149kr) by the canal. Catching the sunset, it's also hugely popular in the evening when there's a French-inspired menu.

CHRISTIANSHAVNS BÅDUDLEJNING

Overgaden Neden Vandet 29 ☎ 32 96 53 53, Ⓦ baadudlejningen.dk. Daily 10am–midnight (evening restaurant is open in summer months only). MAP P.79, POCKET MAP F14

Formerly a boat rental point, this partially covered floating pontoon, moored at the Torvegade bridge, is now a trendy lunch spot, serving a few smørrebrød options (from 95kr), a range of colourful seafood salads, plus cold-cut meat platters. Open for dinner, too.

CHRISTIANIA CYKLER

COPENHAGEN STREET FOOD

Papirøen, Trangravsvej 14 ☎ 69 66 95 61,
Ⓦ copenhagenstreetfood.dk. Easter–Oct
Mon–Sat 11am–10pm, Sun 11am–8pm;
Oct–Easter Thurs & Sun noon–9pm, Fri & Sat
noon–10pm. MAP P.79 POCKET MAP G7
This food market has a more
casual feel than Torvehallerne,
where edible goodies from all
around the world are sold from
the waterfront food trucks,
most of it organic and
sustainable.

DAC CAFÉ

Strandgade 27B ☎ 32 57 19 30, Ⓦ dac.dk.
Mon–Fri 11am–5pm, Wed 11am–9pm, Sat &
Sun 10am–5pm. MAP P.79, POCKET MAP F12
Apart from its wonderful
panoramic views DAC's
first-floor café is especially
popular for the elaborate all-day
weekend brunch (175kr), which
includes home-made gravlax
and waffles.

KADEAU

Wildersgade 10B ☎ 33 25 22 23, Ⓦ kadeau
.dk. Tues & Wed 6pm–midnight, Thurs–Sat
noon–1.30pm & 6pm–midnight. MAP P.79,
POCKET MAP E14
Inspired by the Baltic isle of
Bornholm – in both food and
the art on display – *Kadeau* has
had a Michelin star since 2013.
Its inventive dishes include
locally sourced octopus,
beetroot and pork belly, as well

as indigenous grains and
berries. The "Bornholmerbank"
blowout menu of twenty small
servings costs 1300kr.

KAFFI

Vestmannagade 4 ☎ 32 96 02 20. Mon, Tues
& Sun 8am–3pm, Wed & Thurs 8am–5pm,
Fri 8am–9pm, Sat 9am–6pm. MAP P.79,
POCKET MAP F8
"Kaffi", which means coffee in
Icelandic, prides itself on
exceptionally good coffee.

LAGKAGEHUSET

Torvegade 45 ☎ 32 57 36 07, Ⓦ lagkagehuset
.dk. Mon–Thurs & Sat & Sun 6am–7pm, Fri
6am–7.30pm. MAP P.79, POCKET MAP F14
The original *Lagkagehuset*
(there are now branches across
the city), "Layercake House"
(see p.78) is an exceptional
bakery-cum-patisserie serving
beautiful pastries (from 25kr).

MORGENSTEDET

Fabriksområdet 134, Christiania
Ⓦ morgenstedet.dk. Tues–Sun noon–9pm.
MAP P.79, POCKET MAP H8
Small, welcoming vegetarian
place set in a cute little cottage
that once belonged to the army,
with tables outside in a
peaceful garden. Inexpensive
organic food includes a hot
meal of the day, such as bean
stew or potato gratin (80kr),
and a selection of salads (30kr).

SPICEY KITCHEN CAFÉ

Torvegade 56 ☎ 32 95 28 29. Mon–Sat 5pm–1am, Sun 2–11pm. MAP P.79. POCKET MAP F14

Chaotic, always busy Middle Eastern café dishing up delicious and excellent-value South Asian and Middle Eastern meals – mainly curries and kebabs, with at least one vegetarian option. Prices start at 75kr for a main course.

SPISELOPPEN

Prinsessegade 1, Christiania ☎ 32 57 95 58. Ⓦ spiseloppen.dk. Tues–Sat 5–10pm, Sun 5–9pm. MAP P.79. POCKET MAP G8

Considering the ramshackle staircase leading up to it, the high quality of the cuisine offered by this rustic Christiania collective comes as quite a surprise. The global reach of the menu reflects the wide origins of its chefs.

VIVA

Langebrogade Kaj 570 ☎ 27 25 05 05. Ⓦ restaurantviva.dk. Tues–Sun 5.30pm– midnight (last sitting 9.30pm). MAP P.79. POCKET MAP D14

This small and intimate boat restaurant, moored next to Langebro bridge, serves up an exquisite gourmet six-course tasting menu (400kr) as well as picnic baskets to go, plus wine menu (300kr). Don't miss a preprandial cocktail or *digestif* on the rooftop deck for a magical view of the city lights reflecting in the water.

Bars

HALVANDET

Refshalevej 325 ☎ 70 27 02 96, Ⓦ halvandet .dk. April–Sept 10am till late. MAP P.79. POCKET MAP H4

Located on a disused industrial pier on Holmen, this unusual beach bar is decked out with mattresses (rented for sun-lounging during the daytime), while things get livelier in the evening. Nibbles and light meals are available in the daytime. Best reached via harbour bus or canal boat.

NEMOLAND

Christiania ☎ 32 95 89 31, Ⓦ nemoland.dk. Mon–Thurs 10am–1am, Fri & Sat 10am–3am, Sun 10am–1am. MAP P.79, POCKET MAP G8

This lively café-bar with a large outdoor space is a popular place for visitors to sample purchases from Pusherstreet undisturbed. There are free gigs on a rickety stage outside on summer Sundays, featuring well-known Danish artists and lesser-known international acts.

Music venues

ISLANDS BRYGGES KULTURHUS

Islands Brygge 18 ☎ 33 66 47 00, Ⓦ kulturhusetislandsbrygge.kk.dk. Mon–Wed 10am–11pm, Thurs–Sat 10am–midnight, Sun 10am–10pm. MAP P.79, POCKET MAP E9

The waterfront Islands Brygges Kulturhus puts on a packed programme of gigs, activities (Latin dance on Tuesdays, for example) and film nights. There's also a café-bar-restaurant with a large water-facing terrace out front.

LOPPEN

Christiania ☎ 32 57 84 22, Ⓦ loppen.dk. Gigs most days of the week from 8.30/9pm, see website for details. MAP P.79, POCKET MAP G8

On the first floor of the warehouse that also houses *Spiseloppen* and the Infocaféen this usually tightly packed venue hosts superb live gigs five nights a week. Music ranges from Danish folk to hard-core punk, with admission 50–200kr.

Vesterbro and Frederiksberg

The two neighbouring districts of Vesterbro and Frederiksberg couldn't be more contrasting. Vesterbro was until recently a solidly working-class area. Urban regeneration projects over the past fifteen years have smartened it up, inflating the value of property, and attracting more affluent residents. They have also brought with them a slew of edgy art galleries, restaurants and bars such as those in the über-trendy, newly converted Kødbyen meat-packing area. Conservative Frederiksberg combines elegant tree-lined avenues, beautiful parks and grand villas – a stroll down Frederiksberg Allé to the romantic seventeenth-century Frederiksberg Have (gardens) and palace gives a flavour of its well-heeled opulence. The quaint little street of Værnedamsvej links the two districts with some superb places to eat and drink, exclusive shops and a neighbourly, outgoing feel.

VESTERBROGADE AND ISTEDGADE

MAP OPPOSITE, POCKET MAP B6-E8

As one of the main arteries leading into the city, **Vesterbrogade** has been lined with restaurants and inns since the sixteenth century. Today, it offers access to the hugely popular nightlife of Kødbyen, and retains a bohemian atmosphere thanks to the large number of artists and musicians who still live here. Running roughly parallel, **Istedgade** is all that is left of the city's once infamous red-light district which flourished after the legalization of pornography in the 1960s. Today a handful of hookers and the occasional porn shop near Central Station is all that remains.

VÆRNEDAMSVEJ

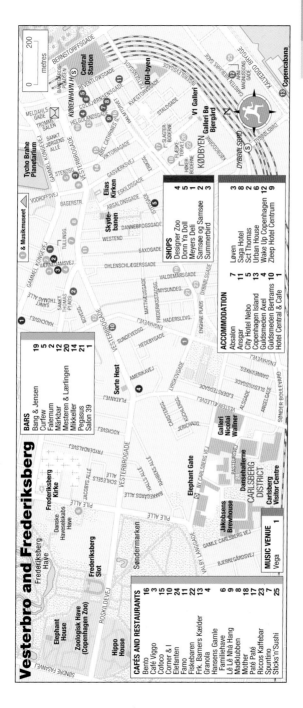

Vesterbro and Frederiksberg

CAFÉS AND RESTAURANTS
Bento	16
Café Viggo	3
Cofoco	15
Corner & I	10
Elefanten	24
Famo	11
Fiskebaren	22
Frk. Barners Kælder	13
Granola	4
Hansens Gamle	
Familiehave	6
Lê Lê Nhà Hang	9
Madklubben	8
Mother	18
Paté Paté	17
Riccos Kaffebar	23
Spuntino	7
Sticks'n'Sushi	25

BARS
Bang & Jensen	19
Curfew	5
Falernum	2
Märkbar	12
Mesteren & Lærlingen	20
Mikkeller	14
Pegasus	21
Salon 39	1

MUSIC VENUE
Vega	1

ACCOMMODATION
Absalon	7
Ansgar	11
City Hotel Nebo	5
Copenhagen Island	13
Guldsmeden Axel	4
Guldsmeden Bertrams	10
Hotel Central & Cafe	1
Løven	3
Saga Hotel	8
Sct Thomas	2
Urban House	6
Wake Up Copenhagen	12
Zleep Hotel Centrum	9

SHOPS
Designer Zoo	4
Dom Ya Doll	5
Meyers Deli	1
Samsøe og Samsøe	2
Summerbird	3

MUSIKMUSEET

Rosenørns Alle 22 ☏ 41 20 63 13,
ⓦnatmus.dk/museerne/musikmuseet.
Tues–Sun 10am–4pm. Free. MAP P87 POCKET
MAP C6

After years in storage, the
many bizarre exhibits of the
Danish museum of music have
finally re-emerged in the
highly appropriate setting of
DR's former radio house, a
modernist building designed
by acclaimed architect Vilhelm
Lauritzen in 1954, close to the
Forum exhibition hall and
metro station. The instruments
on display, which include an
amoeba-shaped violin and
giraffe piano, come from all
four corners of the globe and
date back as far as the 1500s;
there is also the "klang room",
a specially soundproofed room
where children can play their
hearts out without disturbing
the neighbours.

TYCHO BRAHE PLANETARIUM

Gammel Kongevej 10 ☏ 33 12 12 24,
ⓦplanetariet.dk. Mon noon–7.40pm, Tues–
Thurs & Sun 10.30am–7.40pm, Fri & Sat
10.30am–8.50pm. Adults/children under 12
144kr/94kr including IMAX film, 89kr/64kr
without. MAP P.87, POCKET MAP D8

Housed in a massive and
unmissable yellow-brick
cylinder at the foot of Sankt
Jørgens lake, the city's
planetarium is named after
sixteenth-century Danish
astronomer Tycho Brahe. For
many visitors – especially the
local schoolkids who overrun
the place during the week – the
main attraction is the
enormous 3D IMAX screen in
the planetarium's central Space
Theatre, which shows science
and nature films.

KØDBYEN

MAP P.87, POCKET MAP D9

Once Copenhagen's former
meat-packing district,

TYCHO BRAHE PLANETARIUM

Kødbyen is now one of the
trendiest areas in the city. It
encompasses cutting-edge
galleries and arty cocktail bars,
rustic-chic restaurants and
grungy nightclubs, with a vibe
that changes through the day.
Until noon the feel is cold
industrial, with life emanating
only from the few remaining
food-processing plants. After
lunch, the galleries begin to
open and a colourful,
trendsetting crowd moves in.
Come evening the restaurants
pack out with diners and then
partygoers who continue the
evening milling from bar to
bar, and later on into the
nightclubs.

Kødbyen's earliest buildings
– the eastern, "brown" part of
the site – date back to the late
nineteenth century when the
city's slaughterhouses were
focused on one site in a bid to
improve hygiene. The original
indoor cattle market has now
been converted into the
Øksnehallen exhibition centre,
an interesting building with a
vast vaulted ceiling that hosts
regular photography exhibitions as well as trade fairs for
food and fashion, most of them

open to the public. In the 1930s the district was extended with the so-called "white" section to the west, whose functionalist blue-and-white-tile-covered buildings are now protected as an industrial monument.

CARLSBERG VISITOR CENTRE

Gamle Carlsbergvej 11 ☏ 33 27 12 82, Wvisitcarlsberg.dk. Daily 10am–5pm. 85kr. MAP P.87, POCKET MAP B9

Carlsberg's slick visitor centre takes you through the history of the brewery and provides an insight into the interlinked history of Danes and beer. Highlights include the world's largest collection of beer bottles (over 20,000) and a wonderful assortment of old advertising campaigns. Although it lacks the noise and excitement of a large working brewery, you do get the opportunity to sample (alongside regular Carlsberg) some interesting beers from the on-site microbrewery, the **Jacobsen Brewhouse**, at the end of your visit.

The Carlsberg quarter

Exciting developments are well under way on the site of the old Carlsberg Brewery, which moved its production to a new, modern complex in Jutland in 2006. After lengthy public consultation it was decided to develop the site into a vibrant new cultural and residential quarter, **Carlsberg Byen**.

The project is still ongoing, but a number of galleries and cultural institutions have already moved in, such as **Dansehallerne** (Wdansehallerne.dk), a modern-dance performance venue at Tap E (scheduled to move out 2016) and, in the old garages, **Galleri Nicolai Wallner** (Wnicolaiwallner.com), the city's largest private gallery for contemporary art. You could easily spend a half-day exploring the complex. Landmark sights include the iconic **Elephant Gate**, the glorious winding Lotus Chimney, the Lime Tower lighthouse and the Star Gate, the original main entrance to the brewery. Many of Carlsberg's luscious green spaces have also been opened up to the public, including J.C. Jacobsen's tranquil garden next to the *Elefanten* café (p.92).

FREDERIKSBERG HAVE AND SLOT

Roskildevej ⓦ ses.dk. Gardens: 6am–sunset; free. Palace: guided tours Jan–June & Aug–Nov last Sat of the month 11am & 1pm; 50kr. MAP P.87, POCKET MAP A8

One of the city's most beautiful and romantic spots, **Frederiksberg Have** was originally laid out in the late seventeenth century as gardens for the recently completed royal palace. The gardens' Baroque formality was remodelled in the English landscape style a century later, with winding paths weaving across undulating lawns, boating canals and numerous follies hidden among the trees. The park can be accessed from all sides, but arriving from the *slot* gives you the best overview of its layout. Hugely popular for picnicking and lounging, the gardens also host music and theatre performances in summer (check the website for details).

Frederiksberg Slot itself, built in Baroque style, was the royal family's main summer residence until the mid-1800s, and now houses the Danish Officers Academy – it's therefore off-limits except for the infrequent guided tours.

The interior is awash with intricate stuccowork and bold and colourful ceiling paintings; grandest of all is the elaborately decorated chapel, which you may find a little over the top.

ZOOLOGISK HAVE

Roskildevej 32 ⓣ 72 20 02 00, ⓦ zoo.dk. Open from 10am; closing times vary (check website). 170kr, children under 12 95kr. MAP P.87, POCKET MAP A8

Founded in 1859, Copenhagen's **zoological gardens** encompass everything you'd expect from a zoo with over 2500 caged animals from around the globe. Aside from the wooden 44m observation tower (1905), two recently added structures stand out: Foster & Partners' etched-glass-domed **Elephant House**, complete with underfloor heating, and Danish architects Dall & Lindhardsen's **Hippo House**, where you can watch the animals frolic underwater. Both are easily visible from neighbouring parks (Frederiksberg Have for the elephants and Sønder-marken for the hippos), so – should you wish – you can avoid forking out the entrance fee to view them.

ZOOLOGISK HAVE

Shops

DESIGNER ZOO

Vesterbrogade 137 ☎ 33 24 94 93, 🌐 dzoo.
dk. Mon–Thurs 10am–5.30pm, Fri 10am–
7pm, Sat 10am–3pm. MAP P.87, POCKET MAP B8

Welcoming store run by eight
designers selling own-made
furniture, jewellery, knitwear,
pottery and glass. A great place
for that elusive Christmas gift.

DONN YA DOLL

Istedgade 55 ☎ 33 22 66 35, 🌐 donnyadoll
.dk. Mon–Fri 11am–6pm, Sat 10am–3pm.
MAP P.87, POCKET MAP D8

This chaotic clothes shop sells
sustainably produced clothes,
from bamboo underwear to
soya shirts including items
made by top Danish designers
such as Stig P and Eco Nord.

MEYERS DELI

Gammel Kongevej 107 ☎ 33 25 45 95,
🌐 meyersmad.dk. Daily 9am–9pm.
MAP P.87, POCKET MAP C7

The original branch of what is
now a chain, selling delicious
home-made bread as well as
delicacies like honey-cured
ham, home-made pâtés, pickles
and chutneys, and freshly
pressed apple juice.

SAMSØE OG SAMSØE

Værnedamsvej 12 ☎ 35 28 51 02, 🌐 samsoe
.com. Mon–Thurs 10am–6pm, Fri 10am–7pm,
Sat 10am–4pm. MAP P.87, POCKET MAP C8

Cool own-brand designer wear
for men and women, plus a few
items from other labels. They're
known for their simple, loose-
fitting style and punchy colours.

SUMMERBIRD

Værnedamsvej 9 ☎ 33 25 25 50,
🌐 summerbird.dk. Mon–Fri 11am–6pm, Sat
10am–3pm. MAP P.87, POCKET MAP C8

Dinky little chocolatier selling
arguably the world's best
chocolate. Try the otherworldly

MEYERS DELI

flødeboller (cream buns) –
fluffy, chocolate-coated
marshmallow treats.

Cafés and restaurants

BENTO

Helgolandsgade 16 ☎ 88 71 46 46, 🌐 uki.dk.
Tues–Sat 11am–2pm, 5–10pm. MAP P.87,
POCKET MAP D8

Family-run Japanese eatery
with a traditional minimalist
interior. Famous for its
makunouchi (bento) boxes –
from 298kr – it also excels in
less pricey sushi and maki rolls,
and has a well-stocked Japanese
cocktail bar. Takeaway available.

CAFÉ VIGGO

Værnedamsvej 15 ☎ 33 31 18 21,
🌐 cafeviggo.com. Mon–Wed 10am–midnight,
Thurs 10am–1am, Fri 10am–2am, Sat
11am–2am. MAP P.87, POCKET MAP C8

Named after Belgian comic-
book character Gaston (Vakse
Viggo in Danish), this
French-style café-bistro is
packed both day and night.
Apart from good, solid bistro
dishes such as quiche forestière
or steak haché, the chef excels
in genuine Breton *galettes*.

COFOCO

Abel Cathrines Gade 7 ☎ 33 13 60 60, ⓦcofoco.dk. Daily 5.30pm–midnight. MAP P.87, POCKET MAP D8

Bright and modern, *Cofoco* sources much of its food from the Baltic island of Bornholm – where the growing season is longer and produce consequently tastier. Dishes are superb but small (75–85kr), the idea being that you sample a range.

CORNER & I

Helgolandsgade 2 ☎ 33 24 58 58. Daily noon–11pm. MAP P.87, POCKET MAP D8

Plain and verging on stark, the decor here feels almost as authentically Chinese as the home-style food. Try the home-made dim sum (48kr/ portion).

ELEFANTEN

Pasteursvej 20 ☎ 88 81 08 11, ⓦcafeelefanten .dk. Mon–Wed 10am–10pm, Thurs–Sat 10am–11pm, Sun 10am–5pm. MAP P.87, POCKET MAP B9

Housed in Tap E along with *Dansehallerne* (see box, p.89), *Elefanten* is an essential pit stop in the up-and-coming Carlsberg district. Lunch includes smørrebrød (65kr) and sandwiches (85kr), while the short evening menu hinges on hearty meat dishes and lighter pastas or risottos. Sit either in the industrial pillared hall or outside facing J.C. Jakobsen's garden.

FAMO

Saxogade 3 ☎ 33 23 22 50, ⓦfamo.dk. Daily 6pm–midnight. MAP P.87, POCKET MAP C8

Small, cheerful, no-frills Italian restaurant serving a four-course menu (370kr), prepared by a pair of Michelin-starred chefs who have decided to go it alone. Flavour-packed delicacies might include *panzanella* (Florentine bread-and-tomato salad,

crammed with anchovies and herbs) and *ribolita* (Tuscan bean soup).

FISKEBAREN

Flæsketorvet 100 ☎ 32 15 56 56, ⓦfiskebaren .dk. Mon–Thurs 5.30pm–midnight, Fri until 2am, Sat noon–4pm & 5.30pm–2am, Sun noon–4pm & 5.30–11pm. MAP P.87, POCKET MAP D9

This super-trendy fish restaurant in hip Kødbyen offers sustainably sourced fresh fish and seafood, from oysters (costing from 95kr for three) to Greenland snowcrab (165kr), the menu varying according to the season and catch. With whitewashed walls and shiny black floors, it's also a monument to cool industrial chic.

FRK. BARNERS KÆLDER

Helgolandsgade 8 ☎ 33 33 05 33, ⓦfrkbarners.dk. Daily noon–4pm & 5.30–11pm. MAP P.87, POCKET MAP D8

With outdoor seating on a streetside terrace and a cosy cavern-like atmosphere inside, this traditional restaurant – complete with red-and-white-check tablecloths – serves time-honoured Danish classics such as herring platters (98kr) at lunch, and *hakkebøf* (Danish burger) with potatoes, cucumber salad and fried egg (154kr) at dinnertime.

GRANOLA

Værnedamsvej 5 ☎ 31 31 15 36. Mon–Fri 7am–midnight, Sat 9am–midnight, Sun 9am–4pm. MAP P.87, POCKET MAP C8

Retro-style milkshake bar whose decor – including genuine 1930s ceiling lamps from the Rover factory – shows staggering attention to detail. Breakfast (90–165kr, depending on size), smoothies and juices are served from early morning, while later on the menu centres on well-prepared home-made dishes such as quiches, salads, sandwiches – and delicious milkshakes, of course.

HANSENS GAMLE FAMILIEHAVE

Pile Alle 10 ☎ 36 30 92 57, ⓦ hansenshave .dk. April–Sept 11am–midnight, rest of the year Sun until 6pm. MAP P.87, POCKET MAP B8

In a pretty garden (with a retractable winter roof) around the corner from Frederiksberg Slot this popular place excels in smørrebrød (herring 59kr). There's also a good range of traditional hot dishes such as fried eel with parsley sauce (239kr), and roast pork with pickled red cabbage.

LÊ LÊ NHÀ HANG

Vesterbrogade 40 ☎ 33 31 31 25, ⓦ lele.dk. Mon–Thurs 5–10pm, Fri & Sat 5–10.30pm. MAP P.87, POCKET MAP D8

This spacious Vietnamese place serves gorgeous dishes which you can watch being lovingly prepared in the large open kitchen. Try for instance the Saigonese papaya salad with beef and Vietnamese mint (85kr). Takeaway is available further along the street at no. 56 (daily 11.30am–9.30pm).

MADKLUBBEN

Vesterbrogade 62 ☎ 38 41 41 43, ⓦ madklubben.dk. Daily 5.30pm–midnight. MAP P.87, POCKET MAP C8

Simple, well-prepared dishes in a funky, slightly space-age-styled restaurant (part of a small chain) right on the main drag of Vesterbrogade. The straightforward concept (choose from one to four courses, 100–250kr) is a big hit with the Vesterbro crowd. Favourite mains include the fish of the day and the truffle-oil risotto (both cost 100kr).

MOTHER

MOTHER

Høkerboderne 9 ☎ 22 27 58 98, ⓦ mother.dk. Mon–Sat 11am–1am, Sun 11am–11pm. MAP P.87, POCKET MAP D8

Organic sourdough pizza served in a long, rustic butcher's hall in industrial-hip Kødbyen. *Mother*'s chipper Italian proprietor, who also mans the door, is kept busy throughout the day as hungry diners arrive in droves. Pizzas start at 75kr for a filling Marinara. There is a small but select wine list as well as full-flavoured Menabrea beer on draught.

PATÉ PATÉ

Slagterboderne 1 ☎ 39 69 55 57, ⓦ patepate.dk. Mon–Wed 9am–midnight, Thurs 9am–1am, Fri 9am–3am, Sat 11am–3am. MAP P.87, POCKET MAP D8

On-trend Kødbyen wine bar-cum-restaurant housed in a former meat pâté factory. Apart from a vast selection of great wines, *Paté Paté* also offers good, solid French food, with lighter bites on offer at lunchtime and dinner mains, which include onglet steak (185kr) and duck confit (190kr).

RICCOS KAFFEBAR

Istedgade 119 ⓦ riccos.dk. Mon–Fri
8am–11pm, Sat & Sun 9am–11pm. MAP P.87,
POCKET MAP C9

Riccos coffee shops have spread
throughout the city but this is
where it all started, and their
unfaltering passion for good
organic coffee is still in
evidence. Packed into a tight
space with only a few tiny tables
and a long communal bench
along the wall, coffee aficionados cram together here every
morning for their caffeine fix.

SPUNTINO

Vesterbrogade 68 ☎ 70 20 50 89,
ⓦ cofoco.dk. Mon–Sat 5.30pm–midnight.
MAP P.87, POCKET MAP C8

Part of the excellent Cofoco
chain, no-frills *Spuntino* offers
Italian classics such as *arancini*,
braised lamb shank and *panna
cotta*. Mix and match as you
wish (65–100kr/dish) or go for
the recommended five-course
menu (295kr).

STICKS'N'SUSHI

Arni Magnussons Gade 2 ☎ 88 32 95 95,
ⓦ sushi.dk. Mon–Thurs & Sun 10am–11pm, Fri
& Sat 10am–midnight. MAP P.87, POCKET MAP D9

Great-tasting sushi, seafood
salads and Japanese dishes on
the top floor of the twelve-
storey *Tivoli Hotel*, with great
views of Kødbyen and beyond.

Bars

BANG & JENSEN

Istedgade 130 ☎ 33 25 53 18,
ⓦ bangogjensen.dk. Mon–Fri 7.30am–2am,
Sat 10am–2am, Sun 10am–midnight.
MAP P.87, POCKET MAP C8

Housed in an old nineteenth-
century chemist with high
stucco ceilings, *Bang & Jensen*
is a cosy neighbourhood café by
day and a heaving bar at night.
Saturday night features
Ingeborg's Cocktail Salon, when
you can enjoy a daiquiri or dry
martini as the eponymous DJ
spins some ambient tunes.

CURFEW

Stenosgade 1 ☎ 29 29 92 76, ⓦ curfew.dk.
Tues–Thurs 6pm–2am, Fri 4pm–4am, Sat
6pm–4am. MAP P.87 POCKET MAP D8

Lavish cocktail bar inspired by
the speakeasy culture of the
1920s and 1930s, run by
flamboyant Portuguese-born
cocktail aficionado, Humberto
Marques. Also serves tapas.

FALERNUM

FALERNUM

Værnedamsvej 16 ☎ 33 22 30 89,
ⓦfalernum.dk. Mon–Thurs noon–midnight,
Fri & Sat noon–2am, Sun noon–midnight. MAP
P.87, POCKET MAP C8

This snug wood-panelled wine
bar offers most of its wines by
the glass (from 60kr), with
friendly and knowledgeable
waiters on hand to share tasting
notes. There's a wide range of
food served throughout the day,
such as home-made soup and an
outstanding charcuterie platter.

MÄRKBAR

Vesterbrogade 106A ☎ 33 21 23 93.
Tues–Wed 5pm–2am, Thurs–Sat 4pm–5am.
MAP P.87, POCKET MAP C8

Dark, grungy, Berlin-inspired
rock bar with a dependable
crowd of regulars nodding their
heads to the rhythm. A good
range of beer, too.

MESTEREN & LÆRLINGEN

Flæsketorvet 86 ☎ 32 15 24 83. Wed–Sat
8pm–3am. MAP P.87, POCKET MAP D9

Small, worn corner dive in
Kødbyen with a disc-juggling
DJ on Friday and Saturday.
Music ranges from Pink Floyd
to African Soul.

MIKKELLER

Viktoriagade 8 ☎ 33 31 04 15,
ⓦmikkellerdk. Mon–Wed & Sun 1pm–1am,
Thurs & Fri 1pm–2am, Sat noon–2am. MAP
P.87, POCKET MAP D8

Mikkeller is a name whispered
in hushed reverential tones
among the beer cognoscenti,
and this intimate basement bar
is a worthy adjunct to the
serious business of brewing. A
self-declared Carlsberg-Free
Zone, it offers a superb range of
innovative microbrewery ales,
including twenty on tap.

PEGASUS

Mysundegade 28 ☎ 33 31 80 50,
ⓦpegasus-cph.dk. Mon–Thurs 5–11pm, Fri

MIKKELLER

5pm–1am, Sat noon–1am. MAP P.87,
POCKET MAP C9

Friendly and unpretentious,
Pegasus is a cavernous
bodega-type place with outdoor
seating on a peaceful street. It
prides itself on its wide range of
beer and wine, and tasty tapas
to help soak it all up.

SALON 39

Vodroffsvej 39 ☎ 39 20 80 39, ⓦsalon39.dk.
Tues 4–11.30pm, Wed & Thurs 4pm–12.30am,
Fri & Sat 4pm–1.30am.
MAP P.87, POCKET MAP D7

Frederiksberg's first cocktail
bar, this stylish, elegant place
is now also popular for the
meals that accompany the
cocktails – such as, the juicy
39 cheeseburger (149kr).

Music venue

VEGA

Enghavevej 40 ☎ 33 25 70 11, ⓦvega.dk.
MAP P.87, POCKET MAP C9

One of the city's top live
music venues, housing three
stages with sublime sound
featuring well-established artists
and bands through the week.
The attached *Ideal Bar* offers a
slightly lower-key (and much
smaller) venue for catching
up-and-coming local bands
(60–110kr) and DJs.

Nørrebro and Østerbro

Beyond the city ramparts, the two neighbouring mid-nineteenth-century districts of Nørrebro and Østerbro are sometimes difficult to tell apart. This is despite deeply contrasting histories – Nørrebro's one of deprivation and social struggle followed by more recent immigration and gentrification, and Østerbro's characterized by traditional wealth and privilege. Aside from Copenhagen's most famous cemetery they lack standout tourist sights. They do, however, have plenty to offer when it comes to going out and having a good time with the locals. Squares such as trendy Sankt Hans Torv and multicultural Blågårds Plads in Nørrebro, and laidback Bopa Plads in Østerbro, are alive and kicking day and night, as is the once grimy Jægersborgsgade, now one of the city's most hyped streets, thanks mostly to the presence of a Michelin-starred restaurant.

ASSISTENS KIRKEGAARD

Nørrebrogade April–Sept daily 7am–10pm, Oct–March 7am–7pm. Entrances on Nørrebrogade, Jagtvej and Kapelvej. MAP OPPOSITE, POCKET MAP C5

The tranquil leafy cemetery of **Assistens Kirkegaard** was first established in 1760 as a burial place outside the city walls for its poor and destitute. Since then, and especially in the nineteenth century during Copenhagen's Golden Age of art and culture, it became the city's most prestigious and famous burial place. Most of the graves are of the key movers and shakers in the city's past. Pick up one of the colourfully dotted maps at one of the many entrances, each colour representing a profession, and you can make your way around to find graves of luminaries such as author Hans Christian Andersen,

philosopher Søren Kirkegaard, Nobel-prize-winning physicist Niels Bohr and many, many more.

While burials still occasionally take place here, Assistens Kirkegaard has more in common with a regular park with its wide tree-lined cycle paths and picnickers and sunbathers lounging about on warm days, some using the tombstones as back rests.

FÆLLEDPARKEN

MAP P.98, POCKET MAP E3–4

Fælledparken is at half a square kilometre the city's largest park used by over 11 million visitors each year. It started life as a common used to graze the city's livestock. Later it became the favoured haunt for the city's gentlefolk on their Sunday afternoon strolls. Today you'll find all

walks of life here, many of them kicking a ball around one of the six demarcated football pitches. At the corner near Trianglen a tranquil scent garden has been designed for the visually impaired, while across Edel Sauntes Allé, you'll find Northern Europe's largest skatepark, opened in 2012. On sunny days the park becomes a patchwork of sunbathers' blankets and it's often difficult to find a spare patch of grass to settle on. Various events take place in Fælledparken throughout the year. Highlights include May Day and the annual carnival which both culminate here with lots of partying. In front of the park's small café there are also occasional gigs during summer, as well as weekly free Salsa lessons. Check out Ⓦ cafe-pavillonen.dk for details.

BARS		CAFÉS AND RESTAURANTS		MUSIC VENUE	
Antidote	1	Café 22	12	Rust	1
The Barking Dog	8	Floras Kaffebar	17		
Bodega	7	Kaffesalonen	15	**ACCOMMODATION**	
Gefährlich	13	Laundromat	9	Avenue	1
Gilt	18	Manfreds & Vin	2		
N	16	Nørrebro Bryghus	6	**SHOPS**	
Oak Room	5	Relæ	3	Accord	1
Ølbaren	10	Sebastopol	4	Melange de Luxe	5
Props Coffee Shop	14	Søpromenaden	11	Radical Zoo	2
				Ravnsborggade Antique Stores	4
				Stig P	3

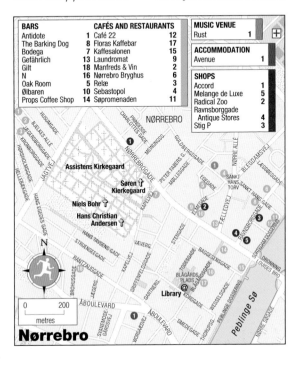

Nørrebro

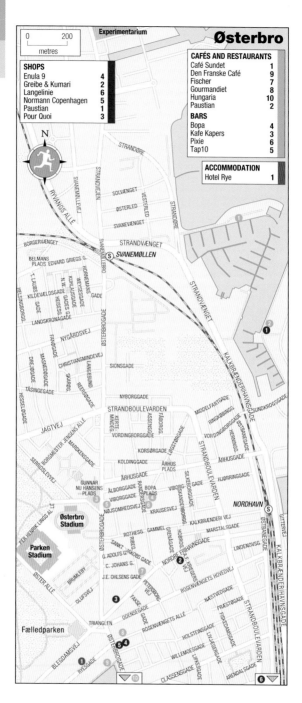

Experimentarium

Østerbro

0   200
metres

SHOPS
Enula 9   4
Greibe & Kumari   2
Langelinie   6
Normann Copenhagen 5
Paustian   1
Pour Quoi   3

CAFÉS AND RESTAURANTS
Café Sundet   1
Den Franske Café   9
Fischer   7
Gourmandiet   8
Hungaria   10
Paustian   2

BARS
Bopa   4
Kafe Kapers   3
Pixie   6
Tap10   5

ACCOMMODATION
Hotel Rye   1

EXPERIMENTARIUM

Tuborg Havnevej 7 ☎39 27 33 33,
Ⓦexperimentarium.dk. April–Oct daily
10am–5pm; Nov–March Mon–Fri 10am–4pm,
Sat & Sun 10am–5pm. 160kr over 11
years/105kr for 3–11 years. MAP OPPOSITE,
POCKET MAP F1

Worth a detour if you have kids,
Experimentarium is a giant
hands-on science lab where you
can test all sorts of things. The
large permanent exhibit looks at
the human body (avoid the
section on sound waves if you
don't like loud noises), how soap
bubbles work, energy generation
and much more. A large
temporary exhibitions space
often features blockbuster
attractions on loan from other
museums. Staff are at hand to
show you what to do, if needed.
Most children are worn out after
a day of running around,
pulling on ropes, pushing

EXPERIMENTARIUM

barrels, leaving parents free to
do what they want afterwards.

At the time of writing the
museum was undergoing
renovation, and had been moved
to Papirøen; the move back to
Hellerup is scheduled late 2016,
check website for details.

Shops

ACCORD

Nørrebrogade 90 ☎70 15 16 17, Ⓦaccord.
dk. Mon–Fri 10am–7pm, Sat 10am–5pm, Sun
noon–5pm. MAP P.97, POCKET MAP C5

This secondhand music store
buys and sells vinyl records, and
is a popular weekend hangout
among forty-something
nostalgists, though there's plenty
here for younger folk too.

ENULA 9

Rosenvængets Allé 6 ☎35 38 17 85,
Ⓦenula9.dk. Mon–Fri 11am–5.30pm, Sat
10am–3pm. MAP OPPOSITE, POCKET MAP F4

Tiny shop selling beautiful
clothes and accessories for
pregnant women and babies.

GREIBE & KUMARI

Norde Frihavnsgade 60 ☎35 55 16 61.
Mon–Fri 11am–5.30pm, Sat 10am–2pm. MAP
OPPOSITE, POCKET MAP F3

Luxury secondhand clothing
store where the richest and most
fashionable of Copenhagen
society drop off their designer
cast-offs. Barely worn examples
of name brands, including
Scandinavian labels Munthe and
Filippa K. Children's clothes too.

LANGELINIE

Langelinie Promenaden Ⓦlangelinie-outlet.dk.
Daily 10am–6pm. MAP OPPOSITE, POCKET MAP G4

A strip of designer outlet stores
– including Noa Noa and
Company's – located along the
pier across from where visiting
cruise ships dock.

MELANGE DE LUXE

Ravnsborggade 6 ☎22 63 65 75, Ⓦmelange
deluxe.dk. Mon–Fri 11am–6pm, Sat 11am–5pm,
Sun noon–4pm. MAP P.97, POCKET MAP D6

Small place selling secondhand
designer wear, including Gucci,
Prada and Chanel, at prices that
don't require a second mortgage.

NORMANN COPENHAGEN

Østerbrogade 70 ☎ 35 27 05 40,
ⓦ normann-copenhagen.com.
Mon–Fri 10am–6pm, Sat 10am–4pm.
MAP P.98, POCKET MAP F4

A showcase for Nordic designer
homeware, with plenty of
high-end pieces as well as a few
quirky and affordable kitchen
accessories. A fun place to see
what cutting-edge creatives can
think of next.

PAUSTIAN

Kalkbrænderiløbskaj 2 ☎ 39 16 65 65,
ⓦ paustian.dk. Mon–Fri 10am–6pm, Sat &
Sun 10am–3pm. MAP P.98, POCKET MAP G2

Superb designer furniture sold
in a magnificent building
designed by Jørn Utzon of
Sydney Opera House fame. The
vast range on offer includes
own-brand furniture as well as
iconic pieces such as Alvar
Aalto sofas and Verner Panton
chairs. There's also a stylish
restaurant (see p.103).

POUR QUOI

Nordre Frihavnsgade 13 ☎ 35 26 62 54,
Mon–Fri 10am–6am, Sat 10am–2pm.
MAP P.98, POCKET MAP F4

Cool clothes for women sold in
a compact three-storey shop
with heaps of fabulous dangly,
glittering accessories. Perfect for
those lusting after leopard-print
leggings or a unique T-shirt.

RADICAL ZOO

Elmegade 19 ☎ 32 14 12 08. Mon–Thurs
11am–6pm, Fri & Sat 11am–7pm. MAP P.97,
POCKET MAP D5

Small basement store selling
achingly on-trend clothes for
men and women from
lesser known Danish and
international designers, plus
some own-brand creations.

RAVNSBORGGADE ANTIQUE STORES

MAP P.97, POCKET MAP D6

The Nørrebrogade end of
Ravnsborggade is famous for
its antique stores. Perusing
these has become a popular
Saturday morning treat and the
prices have skyrocketed as a
consequence. You may still be
able to find some bargains if
you dig around long enough.

STIG P

Ravnsborggade 18 ☎ 35 35 75 00, ⓦ stigp
.dk. Mon–Fri 11am–6pm, Sat 10am–4pm.
MAP P.97, POCKET MAP D5

A minimalist, slimline shop
selling quality ladieswear – own
brand as well as international
names such as Stella
McCartney and Calvin Klein.

Cafés and restaurants

CAFE 22

Sortedams Dosseringen 21 ☎ 35 37 38 27,
ⓦ cafe22.dk. Mon–Wed & Sun
9am–midnight, Thurs–Sat 9am–2am.
MAP P.97, POCKET MAP D5

Tucked away on a quiet corner,
Café 22 is a cosy basement
café-restaurant with a string of
popular lakeside tables with
blankets available when the air

PAUSTIAN

FISCHER

plus some very tasty burgers (around 120kr) served with home-made *frites*.

FISCHER

Victor Borges Plads 12 ☎ 35 42 39 64, Ⓦ hosfischer.dk. Mon–Fri noon–midnight, Sat & Sun 10.30am–midnight. MAP P.98, POCKET MAP F4

Compact and romantic little Italian trattoria in the heart of Østerbro, just off Nordre Frihavnsgade, offering flavour-packed Roman dishes – such as *guancia di maiale con fagioli* (pork cheeks stuffed with cowberries) – a result of the chef's many years of training in Rome. Primi pasta dishes from 125kr; secondi around 235kr.

FLORAS KAFFEBAR

Blågårdsgade 27 ☎ 35 39 00 18, Ⓦ floraskaffebar.dk. Mon 11am–9pm, Tues–Fri 11am–10pm, Sat 10.30am–10pm, Sun 10.30am–9pm. MAP P.97, POCKET MAP D6

Warm and welcoming, *Flora's* is inspired by traditional American coffee shops. The menu features savoury pancakes and home-made chilli (89kr) as well as excellent cakes. Don't miss the scrumptious Valrhona hot chocolate.

GOURMANDIET

Rosenvænget Allé 7A ☎ 39 27 10 00, Ⓦ gourmandiet.dk. Mon–Thurs 11am–6pm, Fri 11am–7pm, Sat 10am–3pm. By night: Thurs–Sat 5.30pm–midnight. MAP P.98, POCKET MAP F4

Gourmandiet is a traditional butcher's shop – evident in the beautiful old tiling – which has evolved into an excellent charcuterie-cum-restaurant. Although open for brunch on Saturdays, and with a lunchtime menu comprising an extensive selection of delicious cold cuts during the week, it's the juicy organic steak three nights a week that's the star attraction.

gets chilly. Busy all day, from breakfast onwards; the good-value menu includes a mouthwatering veggie or meaty brunch (98kr).

CAFÉ SUNDET

Svaneknoppen 2, Svanemøllen ☎ 39 29 30 35, Ⓦ cafesundet.dk. Daily 11am–10pm. MAP P.98, POCKET MAP F1

On the first floor of the Svanemøllen sailing clubhouse with wonderful views of Øresund, *Café Sundet* is the perfect place for a leisurely lunch. The focus is naturally on seafood – such as baked lobster in garlic and basil (132kr) – but you also won't go wrong either with their salads or "light" pizzas (from 50kr).

DEN FRANSKE CAFÉ

Sortedams Dosseringen 101 ☎ 35 42 48 45, Ⓦ denfranskecafe.dk. Mon–Fri 9am–11pm, Sat & Sun 10am–11pm. MAP P.98, POCKET MAP E4

At the posh Østerbro end of the lake, this delightful café with outdoor seating on the lakeside promenade features French-style decor and a few Gallic touches on the menu – freshly baked croissants for example. You'll also find classic Danish rye-bread sandwiches

HUNGARIA

Dag Hammarskjölds Alle 7 ☎ 33 13 91 94, Ⓦ hungaria.dk. Mon–Sat 5.30–11pm. MAP P.98 POCKET MAP F5

Elegant brasserie and wine bar serving the most authentic Hungarian food in Copenhagen, with a lot more than just goulash on the menu. A classic, contemporary take that includes some mouthwatering desserts. Vegetarian options offered – mains start at 185kr.

KAFFESALONEN

Peblinge Dosseringen 6 ☎ 35 35 12 19, Ⓦ kaffesalonen.com. Mon–Fri 8am–midnight, Sat & Sun 10am–midnight. MAP P.97, POCKET MAP D6

An old lakeside favourite which started life as a breakfast/coffee shop for workers on their way home from the nightshift and now offers delicious meals throughout the day, including grilled goat's cheese salad and ribeye steak served with all the trimmings. Weather permitting, service extends to a lakeside pontoon with a lively bar – especially worth dropping by on Midsummer's Eve.

LAUNDROMAT

Elmegade 15 ☎ 35 35 26 72, Ⓦ thelaundromatcafe.com. Mon–Fri 8am–11pm, Sat & Sun 9am–11pm. MAP P.97, POCKET MAP D5

Hugely successful Icelandic concept café which combines laundromat, library and café in one, around the corner from trendy Sankt Hans Torv. Their weekend brunch (138kr) comes recommended, having won several awards, but the place is busy all day with students sipping coffee and people making use of the free wi-fi.

MANFREDS & VIN

Jægersborggade 40 ☎ 36 96 65 93, Ⓦ manfreds.dk. Daily noon–3.30pm & 5.30–10pm. MAP P.97, POCKET MAP C5

New Nordic fine dining in an informal, intimate setting. The food is adventurous featuring ingredients such as duck gizzard and unripe peaches, prepared to perfection in a sharing menu that will set you back 250kr per person. There's also a good-value French-style weekday lunch (five courses for 175kr) and a unique wine list featuring "biodynamic" wines.

NØRREBRO BRYGHUS

Ryesgade 3 ☎ 35 30 05 30, Ⓦ noerrebrobryghus.dk. Mon–Thurs noon–midnight, Fri & Sat noon–2am. MAP P.97, POCKET MAP D5

Microbrewery-cum-restaurant where you can try beer-glazed cauliflower and *panna cotta* served with beer syrup. Surprisingly, it all does seem to work, and the long wood-beamed tables are packed to capacity most nights. Hour-long brewery tours led by the chief brewer (150kr) include four samples en route.

LAUNDROMAT

SEBASTOPOL

PAUSTIAN

Kalkbrænderiløbskaj 2 ☎ 39 18 55 01,
Ⓦ restaurantpaustian.dk. Mon–Fri
10am–6pm, Sat 10am–4pm, Sun
10am–3pm. MAP P.98, POCKET MAP G2

Buzzy restaurant attached to
the top-of-the-range designer
furniture store (see p.100).
The lunchtime menu of
herring, smørrebrød and
salads (from 95kr) provides a
delicious break from furniture
perusing.

RELÆ

Jægersborggade 41 ☎ 36 96 66 09,
Ⓦ restaurant-relae.dk. Wed–Fri 5.30–10pm,
Sat noon-1.30pm & 5.30–10pm. MAP P.97,
POCKET MAP C5

Probably the only Michelin-
starred restaurant in
Copenhagen that won't break
the bank (the four-course
tasting menu costs 450kr).
Expect unusual Nordic fusion
food such as carrots,
elderflower and sesame. The
emphasis is on the dining
experience and you may end
up squeezed a little tight in
this unpretentious basement
restaurant. Reserve a table
well in advance – there are
also a few counter settings
facing the kitchen available at
short notice.

SEBASTOPOL

Sankt Hans Torv 32 ☎ 35 36 30 02,
Ⓦ sebastopol.dk. Mon–Thurs 8am–midnight,
Fri 8am–1am, Sat 9am–1am, Sun 9am–10pm.
MAP P.97, POCKET MAP D5

A Copenhagen fixture since
1994, *Sebastopol* offers a touch
of Parisian café chic on trendy
Sankt Hans Torv. It's often
packed with arty Nørrebro
types indulging in a leisurely
brunch (from 90kr). Later in
the day the French bistro menu
includes dishes such as calf
ragoût or *moules frites* (170kr).
With south-facing seating
outside on the square,
Sebastopol is also a popular
place for a sundowner drink.

SØPROMENADEN

Sortedam Dosseringen 103 ☎ 35 42 66 06,
Ⓦ søpromenaden.dk. Daily 11am–11pm.
MAP P.97, POCKET MAP D5

With checked tablecloths and a
lovely lakeside setting,
Søpromenaden emanates rural
charm even though it's at the
lake's busy and chic Østerbro
end. Menu highlights include
an extensive lunchtime
smørrebrød list and all-time
Danish classics such as
frikadeller and *rødkål* –
meatballs served with pickled
red cabbage (149kr).

103

Bars

ANTIDOTE

Jægersborggade 56 ☎ 38 11 30 30, Ⓦ antidotevinbar.dk. Mon–Tues 4–11pm, Wed & Thurs 4pm–midnight, Fri noon–midnight, Sat 10am–midnight, Sun 10am–11pm. MAP P.97 POCKET MAP C5

Located on uber-trendy foodie street Jægersborggade and owned by the man behind *Bibendum* (p.77), the cure offered by *Antidote* wine bar is in the form of choice wines and American-inspired comfort food, served outside in summer.

THE BARKING DOG

Sankt Hans Gade 19 ☎ 35 36 16 00, Ⓦ thebarkingdog.dk. Mon & Sun 4pm–midnight, Tues–Thurs 4pm–1am, Fri & Sat 4pm–2am. MAP P.97, POCKET MAP D5

When you've had enough of the city's uber-stylish offerings this relaxed neighbourhood pub may come in handy. Featuring a small selection of beers (including a few from Nørrebros Bryghus) and wine, *The Barking Dog* also makes a mean Power's Sour cocktail; ask the waiter for the story.

BODEGA

Kapelvej 1 ☎ 35 39 07 07, Ⓦ bodega.dk. Mon–Thurs 10am–midnight, Fri & Sat 10am–3am, Sun 10am–9pm. MAP P.97, POCKET MAP D5

Charming neighbourhood bar-restaurant facing the yellow-brick walls of the Assistens Cemetery. Sup on some wonderful craft beers (many from Nørrebros Bryghus), good food and awesome hot chocolate during the day. Things get lively on Friday and Saturday evenings when the DJ hits the decks.

BOPA

Løgstørgade 8 ☎ 35 43 05 66, Ⓦ cafebopa .dk. Mon–Wed 9am–midnight, Thurs 9am–2am, Fri 9am–5am, Sat 10am–5am, Sun 10am–midnight. MAP P.98, POCKET MAP F3

Cosy café-bar which gets packed most weekends after 11.30pm when a DJ hits the turntables. Excellent range of beers including some from the Skovlyst Brewery north of the city which uses quirky ingredients such as nettles and beech syrup for flavouring.

GEFÄHRLICH

Fælledvej 7 ☎ 35 24 13 24, Ⓦ gefahrlich .dk. Wed & Thurs 5.30–10.30pm, Fri & Sat 5pm–4am. MAP P.97, POCKET MAP D5

Berlinesque café, restaurant, cocktail bar and nightclub in one (oh, and a hairdressers, too). Once service finishes at the restaurant, the cocktail waiters take over, and the DJ cranks up some floor fillers (club slogan: "fuck you if you can't dance").

GILT

Rantzausgade 39 ☎ 27 26 80 70, Ⓦ gilt.dk. Wed & Thurs 6pm–1am, Fri & Sat 6pm–2am. MAP P.97, POCKET MAP C6

"Honest and unadulterated classic cocktails" goes the sales pitch at this stylish little bar. While you might persuade them to knock up a martini, the emphasis here is on Nordic-inspired concoctions using unusual ingredients such as dandelion syrup and roasted pine needles.

KAFE KAPERS

Gunnar Nu Hansens Plads 2 ☎ 35 25 11 20, Ⓦ kafekapers.dk. Mon–Thurs & Sun 9am–midnight, Fri & Sat 9am–1am. MAP P.98, POCKET MAP E3

On a square a short walk from Fælledparken (p.97), *Kapers* is basically a glass cube encased in a large marquee. The outdoor seating area is a popular place to watch the world go by throughout the year (heaters and blankets provided in winter).

Don't expect conversation to drift far from the favoured subject – brews from around the globe – and you'll be fine. Featuring over one hundred different labels, there's plenty to talk about.

PIXIE

Løgstørgade 2 ☎ 39 30 03 05, ⓦ cafepixie .dk. Mon–Thurs 8am–1am, Fri 8am–4am, Sat 10am–4am, Sun 10am–11pm. MAP P.98, POCKET MAP F3

Facing a small playground on Bopa Plads, *Pixie* is an authentic neighbourhood café (breakfasts from 50kr), popular with parents relaxing on the outdoor terrace. Occasional live music in the evenings.

PROPS COFFEE SHOP

Blågårdsgade 5 ☎ 35 36 99 55, ⓦ propscoffeeshop.dk. MAP P.97, POCKET MAP D6

Quirky bar-cum-café with a slightly chaotic, laidback atmosphere. All of its rickety furniture is for sale – look out for the price tag underneath.

TAP10

Østerbrogade 122 ☎ 61 72 44 87. Tues–Thurs & Sun 4–11pm, Fri & Sat 2pm–1am. MAP P.98, POCKET MAP E3

At the top end of Østerbrogade close to Bopa Plads, this trendy basement bar specializes in Nordic craft beers, with more Scandi-brews chalked up on the board than you could imagine, many of them on draught.

Music venue

RUST

Guldbergsgade 8 ☎ 35 24 52 00, ⓦ rust.dk. Wed–Sat 9pm–5am. MAP P.97, POCKET MAP D5

Three floors of live music with edgy, experimental as well as more mainstream acts and a kickass clubbing scene too (40–60kr). Named after Cold War aviator Mathias Rust.

N

Blågårdsgade 17 ☎ 32 15 68 52, ⓦ cafe-n-2200.dk. Mon–Fri 8am–10pm, Sat & Sun 9am–10pm. MAP P.97, POCKET MAP D6

A chilled-out little place with long tables and benches on lively Blågårdsgade and the perfect spot to absorb the day's last rays of sunshine. Drinks on offer include organic beer and wine, and some wonderful freshly made juices.

OAK ROOM

Birkegade 10 ☎ 38 60 38 60, ⓦ oakroom.dk. Wed 7pm–1am, Thurs 7pm–2am, Fri 4pm –4am, Sat 6pm–4am. MAP P.97, POCKET MAP D5

Super-cool, Mad-Men-esque cocktail bar whose sleek interior, designed by cutting-edge architect Kasper Røøn, transports you back to those heady 1960s days of Danish Functionalism. Don't miss the Venezuelan Butterfly (made with passion fruit, mint and rum), the all-time classic.

ØLBAREN

Elmegade 2 ☎ 35 35 45 34, ⓦ oelbaren .dk. Mon 9pm–1am, Tues & Wed 4pm–1am, Thurs 4pm–2am, Fri 3pm–2am, Sat 1pm–2am, Sun 1–11pm. MAP P.97, POCKET MAP D5

A small, bar run for and by beer nerds – and proud of it.

Day-trips

An afternoon away from the big city is essential for getting to know a gentler, quieter Denmark. Copenhagen is just a short train ride or even cycle from some stellar destinations in greater Zealand. If you're staying in town for more than just a day or two, you'll definitely want to venture north on a train (and take your rented cycle with you if you like) for art museums, parklands and castles galore – including the very fortress that inspired Shakespeare's Elsinore Castle in *Hamlet*. South, meanwhile, you'll find beaches, quiet townships, more art and Scandinavia's biggest and best aquarium.

DYREHAVEN AND BAKKEN

Klampenborg S-Tog station. Bakken ☎39 63 35 44, ⓦbakken.dk. End of March to end of Aug daily 9am–5pm & 9am–4.30pm. Admission free; multi-ride pass 249kr, children 179kr. MAP OPPOSITE

A short walk from Klampenborg S-Tog station, the largely forested **Dyrehaven** (Deer Park) was established in 1669 as a royal hunting ground, and is still home to some two thousand (fairly tame) red, sika and fallow deer. It's a picturesque spot, with the ancient oak and beech woodland an atmospheric backdrop, particularly in the early morning mist. Poised on a hilltop in the middle of the park is the **Eremitages-lotten** (Ermitage Palace), a grand hunting lodge built for Christian VI in 1736, though it's closed to the public.

Occupying part of the park's southern section, **Bakken** is supposedly the oldest still-functioning amusement park in the world, tracing its origins back to 1583 when entertainers first set up business next to Kirsten Piil's holy spring. It lacks the polish or refinement of Tivoli – but with 33 rides and almost as many places to drink, there's plenty of fun to be had, not least at weekends when the place can be heaving.

DYREHAVEN

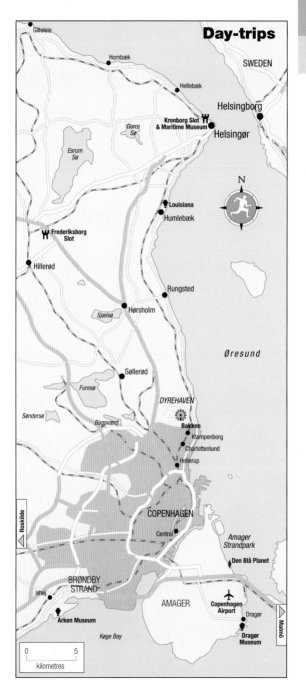

Day-trips

Gilleleie

Hornbæk

Hellebæk

SWEDEN

Helsingborg

Kronborg Slot & Maritime Museum

Helsingør

Gurre Sø

Esrum Sø

N

Louisiana

Humlebæk

Frederiksborg Slot

Hillerød

Rungsted

Sjælsø

Hørsholm

Øresund

Søllerød

Furesø

Søndersø

Bagsværd

DYREHAVEN

Bakken

Klampenborg

Charlottenlund

Hellerup

Roskilde

COPENHAGEN

Central

Amager Strandpark

Den Blå Planet

BRØNDBY STRAND

Malmö

Ishøj

Arken Museum

AMAGER

Copenhagen Airport

Dragør

Dragør Museum

Køge Bay

0   5
kilometres

LOUISIANA

Humlebæk train station, from which it's a 10min walk (follow the signs) ☎ 49 19 07 19, ⓦ louisiana.dk. Tues–Fri 11am–10pm, Sat & Sun 11am–6pm. 115kr. MAP P.107

A perfect fusion of art, architecture and landscape, **Louisiana Museum of Modern Art** – with good reason Denmark's most visited art gallery – has a setting nearly as magical as the museum itself. Overlooking the Øresund strait, the museum began life in 1958, when a series of interconnecting glass pavilions was built around a nineteenth-century villa, Louisiana (named after the original owner's three wives, each of whom, oddly enough, was called Louise) – the ensemble landscaped within an outdoor sculpture park. Louisiana's collection grew quickly and the museum is now home to over three thousand permanent works from around the globe, many world-class.

The entrance is in the main villa, from which – moving clockwise into the west wing – you first reach a light, open space primarily used for temporary shows; exhibitions in recent years have included Andy Warhol, David Hockney, Ai Weiwei and Emil Nolde. Next, housed in a purpose-built gallery, is an outstanding collection of **Giacometti**'s gaunt sculptures and drawings, which leads on to the museum's extensive and colourful collection of abstract works by **CoBrA** (see p.71). Major Danish artists such as Henrik Heerup and Asger Jorn – who has a special room dedicated to his art – are featured alongside.

From the museum café, with its outdoor terrace overlooking Øresund, a subterranean section of graphic art leads onto another of the museum's highlights, the permanent exhibition in the museum's south wing, which focuses on **Constructivism** with works by the likes of Vasarely, Albers and Soto. **Nouveau Réalisme** is represented with pieces by Yves Klein, César and Raysse among others, while Lichtenstein, Rauschenberg, Warhol and Oldenburg lead the charge for the **Pop Art** and **Minimalism** collections.

Outside, on the lawns sloping down towards the coast, the **sculpture garden** is home to around sixty works including Max Ernst, Henri Laurens, Miró and Henry Moore.

LOUISIANA

FREDERIKSBORG SLOT

S-Tog line E to Hillerød, then bus #301 to Ullerød or #302 to Sophienlund ☎ 48 26 04 39, ⓦ dnm.dk. Daily April–Oct 10am–5pm; Nov–March 11am–3pm. 75kr. MAP P.107

Glorious **Frederiksborg Slot** lies decorously across three small islands within an artificial lake, and is set within magnificent Baroque gardens. It was originally the home of Frederik II and birthplace of his son Christian IV, who, at the beginning of the seventeenth century, had it rebuilt in an unorthodox Dutch Renaissance style. It's the unusual aspects of the design – a prolific use of towers and spires, Gothic arches and flowery window ornamentation – that still stand out.

Since 1882, the interior has functioned as a **Museum of National History** with sixty-odd rooms charting Danish history since 1500. Many are surprisingly free of furniture and household objects, drawing attention instead to the ranks of portraits along the walls – a motley crew of flat-faced kings and thin consorts who between them ruled and misruled Denmark for centuries.

KRONBORG SLOT

Helsingør train station, from which it's a 15min walk ☎ 49 21 30 78, ⓦ kronborg.dk. Easter–May & Sept & Oct daily 11am–4pm; June–Aug daily 10am–5.30pm; Nov–Easter Tues–Sun 11am–4pm. 90kr. Guided tours of the royal chambers in English daily at 11.30am and 1.30pm; of the casemates daily 12.30pm. MAP P.107

Tactically placed on a sandy curl of land extending seawards into the Øresund some 45km north of Copenhagen in the city of Helsingør, **Kronborg Slot** is impossible to miss. It's known primarily – under the name of Elsinore Castle – as

the setting for Shakespeare's *Hamlet*, though it's uncertain whether the playwright actually ever visited Helsingør.

Constructed in the fifteenth century by Erik of Pomerania, the original fortress of Krogen was for hundreds of years the key to control of the Øresund (Helsingborg on the other side of the strait was also under Danish rule), enabling the Danish monarchs to extract a toll from every ship that passed through it.

MARITIME MUSEUM OF DENMARK

Kronborg Slot ☎ 49 21 06 85, ⓦ mfs.dk. July & Aug daily 10am–5pm; Sept–June Tues–Sun 11am–5pm. 110kr. MAP P.107

Denmark's newest museum is set underground in the old dry docks next to Kronborg Castle. Built at a cost of 13 million kroner and opened in mid-2013, the structure comprises a continuous ramp looping around the dock walls, allowing for unobstructed views of the castle. Inside, informative and interactive exhibits span Viking, medieval and modern seafaring, exploration and merchant shipping (including a colossal Maersk freight container).

DEN BLÅ PLANET

AMAGER STRANDPARK

Metro to Øresund Station or bus #77 or #78
Ⓦ 33 66 33 19. MAP P.107

Just to the southeast of the centre of Copenhagen, beyond Christianshavn, is the large island of **Amager**. On its east coast, with fine views of the Øresunds Bridge, **Amager Strandpark** is one of the city's most popular summer getaways, with around 5km of beautiful, soft sandy beaches. The beautifully restored traditional wooden **Helgoland Søbadean-stalt**, where Øresundsvej meets Amager Strandvej, offers free changing facilities and showers (late June to end of Aug; free), while at the southern end, **Kastrup Søbad** (June to mid-Sept Mon–Fri 3–10pm, Sat & Sun 11am–10pm; free) has a 5m-high trampoline which provides a fabulous launch pad into the water.

Connected to "mainland" Amager by three short bridges is an artificial island some 2km long, with a shallow lagoon, popular for kitesurfing, windsurfing and kayaking and ideal for kids to paddle in. There are toilets and showers all along the beach, and at its southern end a couple of good places to eat (see p.112).

DEN BLÅ PLANET

Metro to Kastrup Station, from which it's a 10min walk Ⓣ 44 22 22 44, Ⓦ www .denblaaplanet.dk. Mon 10am–9pm, Tues–Sun 10am–6pm. 169kr, children 3–11yrs 95kr. MAP P.107

In a spectacular waterside position next to Kastrup marina, **Den Blå Planet** (The Blue Planet) was opened in 2013 to provide a state-of-the-art new home for Denmark's National Aquarium. All curves, it's a remarkable structure, shaped – when viewed from the air – like a giant whirlpool, with five "arms" radiating from the vortex centre, a circular foyer. Each arm represents a different environment: habitats range from a sunken Amazon forest, featuring Europe's largest school of piranhas, to a Faroese bird cliff, complete with puffins and divers. Highlight for many, though, is undoubtedly the walk through the huge "ocean" aquarium tunnel, with hammerhead sharks and manta rays swimming above and below you and inquisitive sea lions pressing up to the glass. The building has already won several design awards, and is among the best spots in the city to cut loose (and curry favour with) the kids for an afternoon.

ARKEN MUSEUM OF MODERN ART

Train to Ishøj station, then bus #128 (10min), or a 20min walk ☎ 43 54 02 22, ⓦ www.arken.dk. Tues & Thurs–Sun 10am–5pm, Wed 10am–9pm. 95kr. MAP P.107

Smaller and more manageable than Louisiana or the Statens Museum for Kunst, the **Arken Museum for Moderne Kunst** (Arken Museum of Modern Art), just outside the coastal town of Ishøj about 20km southwest of Copenhagen, is well worth seeking out both for its architecture and for its content. Paying homage to its bleak position in front of a windswept sandy beach, architect Søren Robert Lund designed the museum to resemble a shipwreck, its prow thrusting dramatically up from among the dunes. The museum is known for its excellent temporary exhibitions – recent shows have covered eco architect Hundertwasser and Danish artist of the 1920s and 1930s, Gerda Wegener– though these merely supplement a permanent display that focuses on contemporary art from the 1990s onwards and includes pieces by Damien Hirst, Antony Gormley, Jeff Koons and Grayson Perry as well as Danish artists Per Kirkeby and Asger Jorn. Its café is also well worth a visit (see p.112).

DRAGØR

Tårnby Station, then bus #350S to the end. Museum: ☎ 30 10 88 68, ⓦ www .museumamager.dk. May & Sept Sat & Sun noon–4pm; June & end Aug Thurs–Sun noon–4pm; July to mid-Aug Tues–Sun noon–4pm. 40kr, children free. MAP P.107

South of Copenhagen Airport, in the southeasternmost corner of Amager, lies the atmospheric cobblestoned fishing village of **Dragør**, formerly the departure point for ferries to Sweden. It now mainly survives on tourism and the high incomes of its city-commuting inhabitants – properties in Dragør do not come cheap. Apart from meandering around the quaint streets, and lazing on the peaceful south coast beaches, while here you could check out the **Dragør Museum**, devoted to the maritime history of the village from the thirteenth-century herring trade to the arrival of the Dutch in the early sixteenth century.

Rocking Roskilde

The carnivalesque **Roskilde festival** (ⓦwww.roskilde-festival .com) might be Europe's single best open-air event, commonly drawing some 100,000 people. At the end of June, throngs of Danish teens, kidults and ageing hipsters descend on a Roskilde farm to hear more than 150 Scandinavian and international acts take to the eight stages. Pharrell Williams and Paul McCartney were recent performers, but Roskilde is best for lesser-known acts. Logistically it's surprisingly efficient, with free camping next to the festival site and shuttle buses from the train station. Tickets are priced around 2000kr and regularly sell out, so plan in advance.

Roskilde (30min by train from Copenhagen) was thus the obvious location for **Denmark's Rock Museum**, which opened in the vibrant Musicon district at the end of 2015. Also worth a look is the **Viking Ship Museum** (daily 10am–4pm/5pm in summer; 115kr; ⓦvikingeskibsmuseet .dk), home to five well-preserved Viking longships. In summer you can row a modern version in the harbour.

Cafés and restaurants

ALLEHÅNDE

Havkajakvej 16, Amager Strandpark
☎ 53 60 30 38, ⓦ allehaandecafe.dk.
June–Aug daily 11am–5pm, later when there
are events.

A modern houseboat in a fine setting on Amager Strandpark, *Allehånde* ("Allspice") offers tapas (45kr per tapa) to die for – make your choice from a list of options on a blackboard – and first-rate sandwiches (grilled veg and hummus 65kr). It's manned by hearing-impaired staff (with an interpreter) and run by a social foundation that aims to guide them into permanent employment.

ARKEN MUSEUM CAFÉ

Skovvej 100, Ishøj ☎ 51 67 02 23,
ⓦ arken.dk. Tues & Thurs–Sun 10am–4.30pm,
Wed 10am–8.30pm.

Beautiful herring platters (139kr) and sandwiches served in an elegant café upstairs in the museum, with sweeping views of marram-grass-covered dunes and the deep blue sea in the distance. The menu also includes a handful of tasty hot dishes – baked cod with kale, for instance –and the obligatorily excellent cake (35kr).

CAFÉ KYSTENS PERLE

Bryggergården 14, Kastrup ☎ 32 50 40 19,
ⓦ cafekystensperle.dk. Mon–Fri 11am–10pm,
Sat & Sun 10am–10pm.

A short walk from Den Blå Planet, this striking eighteenth-century restaurant was once a brewery. With its crooked walls and low ceilings the "Pearl of the Coast" has retained some of its old-fashioned ambience while its front terrace provides

ARKEN MUSEUM CAFÉ

great coastal views. Food is served throughout the day, including brunch (fruit platter 45kr), a lunchtime smørrebrød platter (139kr) and burgers (135kr) and steak later in the day.

CAFÉ SYLTEN

Søndre Strandvej 50, Dragør ☎ 30 50 60 19,
ⓦ sylten.dk. Mon–Fri noon–11pm, Sat & Sun
11am–11pm.

Hidden away among the dunes a stone's throw from the beach just south of Dragør, this old dark-wood cabin is a wonderful place to catch the sunset on a summer evening. Come for a drink on the terrace (there's a small but select beer and wine list) or to sample some hearty meat dishes (from 150kr). At weekends there's a brunch buffet (179kr; 11am–2pm).

DRAGØR RØGERI

Gammel Havn 6–8, Dragør ☎ 32 53 06 03,
ⓦ dragor-rogeri.dk. Thurs–Sun 10am–4pm.

Authentic smokehouse at Dragør harbour that sells an enormous array of freshly caught and freshly smoked seafood, including legendary smoked eel and herring. They're suppliers to the main restaurants in the city but you can cut out the middleman and enjoy their home-made *fiskefrikadeller og remoulade* (fishcakes with tartare sauce) or fried plaice and chips (both 55kr) at their harbourfront picnic table for half the price.

PETER LIEPS HUS

Dyrehaven 8 ☎ 39 64 07 86, ⓦ peterliep.dk. Tues–Sun 11am–5pm.

Quaint thatched restaurant on a busy pedestrian junction at the edge of Dyrehaven woods, not far from the Bakken amusement park. Lunch at *Peter Lieps* is a popular weekend treat for busy city folk, with a menu focusing primarily on smørrebrød – with an extensive list of over twenty toppings – and classics such as a delicious venison burger made with local game. Mains are in the 150–250kr range.

RESTAURANT PIIL & CO

Dyrehaven 7, Klampenborg ☎ 70 26 02 12, ⓦ piil-co.dk. Daily noon–5pm.

Tucked away in Dyrehaven next to the famous holy spring of Kirsten Piil and overlooking a lake, this romantic log cabin is a great place for pancakes and hot chocolate after a day in the woods. For more substantial dining there is also an excellent lunchtime spread of smørrebrød classics and a few à la carte dishes such as saddle of pork with apple and crackling (125kr). Just a ten-minute walk from Klampenborg station.

SPISESTEDET LEONORA

Frederiksborg Slot, Møntportevej 2, Hillerød ☎ 48 26 75 16, ⓦ leonora.dk. Daily: April–Sept 10am–5pm; Oct–March 10am–3.30pm.

Housed in one of Frederiksborg Slot's former stables, with seating outside in the palace courtyard in summertime, *Leonora* serves a traditional Danish lunch that's fit for a king. Lavishly presented smørrebrød, tartlets overflowing with asparagus and chicken, fillets of plaice served with prawns and caviar, all very reasonably priced.

Bar

SKY BAR

Bella Sky Comwell Hotel, Ørestaden. Take metro to Bella Center or bus #30 from Vesterport ☎ 32 47 30 00, ⓦ bellaskycomwell .dk. Mon–Thurs noon–1am, Fri & Sat noon–1am, Sun noon–11pm.

On the top floor of the extraordinary *Bella Sky* hotel – a vast, 814-room complex – the *Sky Bar* provides breathtaking views of the city skyline and across to Sweden. It's accessed via the super-cool aerial walkway that links the two twisting leaning towers. Drinks here are worth sampling, too: there's a good selection of champagnes and wines, or a gin and tonic will set you back 95kr.

PETER LIEPS HUS

Malmö

Just a short hop across the water from Copenhagen, the Swedish city of Malmö makes for a tempting day-trip. Once part of Denmark (the Danes spell it "Malmø"), it was acquired by the Swedish king Karl X in 1658 along with Skåne (Scania), the surrounding province. Today Malmö is Sweden's third largest city, an attractive mix of chocolate-box medieval squares and striking modern architecture, most notably the Turning Torso skyscraper, Scandinavia's tallest building. You'll also find it a cosmopolitan, culturally diverse population – more than a hundred languages are spoken on its streets and Turkish and Thai food are as popular as meatballs and herring.

STORTORGET AND LILLA TORG

The city's main square, **Stortorget** is as impressive today as it must have been when it was first laid out in the sixteenth century. It's flanked on one side by the imposing **Rådhus**, built in 1546 and covered with statuary and spiky accoutrements. To its rear stands the fine Gothic **St Petri Kyrka** (daily 10am–6pm; free) while to the south runs **Södergatan**, Malmö's main pedestrianized shopping street.

A late sixteenth-century spin-off from Stortorget, **Lilla Torg** is everyone's favourite part of the city. Lined with cafés and restaurants, it's usually pretty crowded at night, with drinkers kept warm under patio heaters and bars handing out free blankets.

MALMÖHUS CASTLE

Malmöhusvägen ☎ 040 34 44 00, ⊕ malmo.se. Daily 10am–5pm. 40SEK. MAP OPPOSITE.

The princely **Malmöhus** is a low fortified castle defended by a wide moat and two circular keeps. Built by Danish king Christian III in 1536, the castle was later used for a time as a prison, but it now houses the **Malmö Museer**, a disparate but fascinating collection of exhibitions on everything from geology to photography – and an aquarium, too. The pleasant

Visiting Malmö

Frequent **trains** (34min; 90kr) connect Copenhagen with Malmö, across the 16km Öresund Bridge/tunnel link. You arrive in the bowels of Malmö's rebuilt Central Station. **Malmö Airport** is located 30km to the east with frequent bus connections into the city as well as to Copenhagen. The **tourist office**, opposite the train station at Skeppsbron 2 (Mon–Fri 9am–7pm, Sat & Sun 9am–4pm, reduced hours in winter ☎040 34 12 00, ⊕malmotown.com), sells the Malmö City Card (100SEK), a voucher book (also available as an app) offering a range of discounts. Many shops accept Danish kroner though at an uncompetitive 1–1 rate so it's usually best to convert to Swedish currency (SEK).

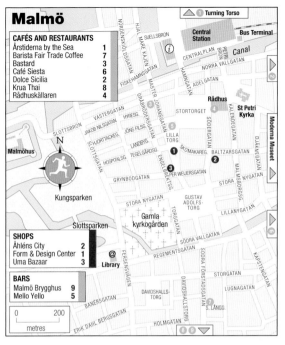

Malmö

CAFÉS AND RESTAURANTS

Årstiderna by the Sea	1
Barista Fair Trade Coffee	7
Bastard	3
Café Siesta	6
Dolce Sicilia	2
Krua Thai	8
Rådhuskällaren	4

SHOPS

Åhléns City	2
Form & Design Center	1
Uma Bazaar	3

BARS

Malmö Brygghus	9
Mello Yello	5

0	200
metres	

grounds, the **Kungsparken**, are peppered with small lakes and an old windmill.

MODERNA MUSÉET

Ola Billgrens plats 2–4 ☎ 040 68 57 937, ⓦ modernamuseet.se. Tues–Sun 11am–6pm. 70SEK. MAP ABOVE.

Opened in 2009, this branch of Stockholm's famous modern art museum hosts excellent temporary exhibitions. The building itself is worth a visit for the striking orange-red cube extension built on to what was the city's electricity works.

THE TURNING TORSO

A good twenty-minute walk or five-minute cycle ride north of the station is Malmö's most iconic sight, the 190m **Turning Torso** skyscraper. A spiralling helix of glass and steel, the structure was completed in 2005 and now lords it over the

sea towards Denmark. Heading coastwards takes you to a viewpoint of the 8km **Öresund Bridge**, the longest road-and-rail bridge in Europe. There's also access to the Ribban, Malmö's artificial sandy beach.

TURNING TORSO

Shops

ÅHLÉNS CITY

Södergatan 15 ☎ 040 24 13 00,
ⓦ ahlens.se. Mon–Fri 10am–8pm, Sat
10am–7pm, Sun 11am–6pm. MAP P.115

Malmö's glitziest department
store, packed with Swedish
designer labels including Acne
and Nudie Jeans.

FORM & DESIGN CENTER

Lilla Torg 9 ☎ 040 664 51 50,
ⓦ formdesigncenter.com. Tues–Sat
11am–5pm, Sun noon–4pm. MAP P.115

This gallery-café-shop has a lot
to offer including a good
selection of Scandinavian
design knick-knacks, and some
handmade items (tea cosies,
candlestick holders and the
like) by local artists.

UMA BAZAAR

Per Wijersgatan 9 ☎ 040 12 30 85,
ⓦ umabazaar.se. Mon–Fri 11am–6pm,
Sat 11am–4pm. MAP P.115

Fair Trade shop that sells
everything from Indian pillows
and African carpets to recycled
jeans and wooden watches.
Being Swedish it's all resolutely
stylish, organic and sustainable.

Cafés and restaurants

ÅRSTIDERNA BY THE SEA

Dockgatan 1 ☎ 040 23 34 88, ⓦ arstiderna
bythesea.se. Mon & Fri 11.30am–2.30pm,
Tues–Thurs 11.30am–9pm. MAP P.115

Large glass-fronted seafood
restaurant located at the marina
in the Western harbour area.
The menu centres on primarily
locally and sustainably sourced
produce such as lovely
pan-fried cod (175SEK) and a
wonderful seafood soup.

BARISTA FAIR TRADE COFFEE

Södra Förstadsgatan 24 ☎ 040 97 26 06,
ⓦ baristafairtrade.com. Mon–Fri 8am–8.30pm,
Sat & Sun 9am–8.30pm. MAP P.115

This award-winning café chain,
now with branches across
Sweden, is the place to head for
coffee snobs. Perfectly poured,
ethically sourced and organic.

BASTARD

Mäster Johansgatan 11 ☎ 040 12 13 18.
ⓦ bastardrestaurant.se. Tues–Thurs 5pm–
midnight, Fri & Sat 5pm–2am. MAP P.115

Yes, you read that right. This
hip gastropub-style restaurant,
run by tattooed young chef
Andreas Dahlberg, has brought
nose-to-tail dining to Malmö,
be it pig cheek, heart, trotters
or tongue. Don't miss the
Bastarrdplanka, a mix of
sausages, hams and pâté served
on a wooden board. Excellent
wines too. Mains from 195SEK.

CAFÉ SIESTA

Hjorttackegatan 1 ☎ 040 611 10 27,
ⓦ siesta.nu. Mon–Thurs 11.30am–11pm, Fri &
Sat 11.30am–12.30am. MAP P.115

Terrific little café, popular for
brunch on weekends when you
can enjoy the likes of smoked
salmon smørrebrød (85SEK)

ÅRSTIDERNA BY THE SEA

and french toast. Evening mains include *moules frites* with organic mussels (170–200 SEK).

DOLCE SICILIA

Drottningtorget 6 ☎ 040 611 31 10, Ⓦ dolcesicilia.se. Daily 11am–7pm (closed Mon and after 5.30pm in winter; open till 8pm in June and July). MAP P.115

A proper Italian-run *gelateria* with delicious organic ice cream made fresh every day, as well as coffee and ciabatta. Also a prime people-watching spot.

KRUA THAI

Möllevångstorget 12 ☎ 040 12 22 87, Ⓦ kruathai.se. Mon 11am–3pm, Tues–Fri 11am–10pm, Sat 1–10pm, Sun 2–10pm. MAP P.115

Affordable, authentic Thai food just south of the centre on Möllevångstorget. Pad Thai 89SEK. Unlicensed.

RÅDHUSKÄLLAREN

Stortorget ☎ 040 79 020, Ⓦ profilrestauranger .se/radhuskallaren. Mon–Wed 11.30am–2pm & 5–10.30pm, Thurs–Sat 11.30am–2pm & 5–11pm, Sun 2–8pm. MAP P.115

Historic restaurant in the vaulted cellar of the town hall, serving a good-value lunch buffet (100SEK including salad, cheese and coffee) and a sophisticated à la carte dinner

menu featuring meaty mains such as pork tenderloin or cajun fried chicken (from 169SEK).

Bars

MALMÖ BRYGGHUS

Bergsgatan 33 ☎ 040 20 96 85, Ⓦ malmo brygghus.se. Mon–Tues 5–11pm, Wed–Thurs 4pm–1am, Fri & Sat noon–3am. MAP P.115

Sup pale ales, pilsners and porters at the city's only microbrewery, a ten-minute walk south of the old centre. The attached pub is open late and on Fridays and Saturdays you can take a tour of the brewery itself (290SEK).

MELLO YELLO

Lilla Torg 1 ☎ 040 30 45 25, Ⓦ melloyello.se. Mon–Fri 3.30pm–1am, Sat & Sun noon–1am. MAP P.115

This stylish bar is the best of the bunch on Lilla Torg. The long cocktail list is supplemented by good draught beers including Brooklyn lager. Food ranges from delicious tapas (139SEK for five dishes) to excellent seafood: try the *Västerbottenpie*, a Swedish speciality with cheese and fish roe.

ACCOMMODATION

Hotels

Hotels do not come cheap in Copenhagen, hovering around the 800–1200kr (£90–130/€110–160) mark for an average double room in high season (late June to early September). Those close to the sights of Tivoli and the Inner City (Indre By) are particularly expensive, while the Vesterbro area is the city's budget hotel district with Helgolandsgade in particular lined with more affordable options. Facilities offered at most places are ultra-modern, boasting fabulous design and eco-concious features in true Danish style. The prices listed below are based on two adults sharing the cheapest en-suite double room in high season inclusive of tax (25 percent). If breakfast costs extra we have indicated this in the review. Online discounts and opting for a shared bathroom can reduce prices significantly.

Tivoli and Rådhuspladsen

CAB-INN CITY > Mitchellsgade 14 📞 33 46 16 16, 🌐 cabinn.com. MAP P.33, POCKET MAP B14. Modern budget hotel around the corner from Central Station and a stone's throw from Tivoli, *Cab-Inn's* main forte – apart from its compact and super-functional ferry-cabin-style rooms – is its central yet relatively quiet location away from the hubbub of Vesterbro. Rooms sleep up to three people. Part of a larger chain with hotels in Frederiksberg (Vodroffsvej 55 and Danasvej 22) and another one in Ørestaden (Arne Jakobsens Allé 2) designed by Daniel Libeskind. Breakfast 70kr. **675kr**

HOTEL NIMB > Bernstorffsgade 5 📞 88 70 00 00, 🌐 hotel.nimb.dk. MAP P.33, POCKET MAP A13. Fairy-tale hotel located upstairs in Tivoli's Moorish-inspired Nimb building from 1909. With just fourteen individually decorated extravagant rooms this is Copenhagen's original boutique hotel. Features include open fireplaces, antique wooden furniture and sweeping views of the gardens. *Hotel Nimb's* opulence encompasses in-room massage (for 1250kr an hour) and a private chauffeur service (1100kr to be picked up at the airport). **30000kr**

HOTEL TWENTYSEVEN > Løngangstræde 27 📞 70 27 56 27, 🌐 firsthotels.com. MAP P.33, POCKET MAP B13. Good-value designer hotel slap bang in the city centre and a minute's walk from the Rådhus (whose bells toll every fifteen minutes until midnight and from 7am in the morning, so worth bearing in mind if you're a light sleeper). With spacious modern rooms and a popular courtyard where cocktails from the hotel's *Honey Ryder* cocktail bar can be devoured. Breakfast 100kr. **1080kr**

PALACE HOTEL > Rådhuspladsen 57 📞 33 14 40 50, 🌐 palacehotel copenhagen.com. MAP P.33, POCKET MAP B12. Wonderful Art Nouveau hotel from 1910 located next door to the Rådhus. A recent refurbishment has reinstated its original decor, featuring lovely details such as George Jensen silver door handles and abstract artwork on the walls. During its heyday many a Hollywood star stayed here including the likes of Audrey Hepburn and Gregory Peck. Although restored to their original appearance, rooms have been totally modernized with comfy beds and luxurious bathrooms. Breakfast included. **1630kr**

RADISSON BLU ROYAL HOTEL >
Hammerichsgade 1 ☎ 33 42 60 00,
ⓦradissonblu.com/royalhotel
-copenhagen. MAP P.33, POCKET
MAP A13. The *Royal Hotel* is an
Arne Jakobsen masterpiece and a
prominent example of Danish modernist
architecture. A twenty-two-storey
rectangular grey and green structure,
the hotel is today graced with his
furniture throughout, including the
famous Swan, Egg, and Drop chairs
which were designed specifically for the
hotel. Although modern luxury abounds,
the hotel today also has a funky
time-warped feeling, not least as you
step into the 1960s lobby. For the full
retro experience book the Arne Jacobsen
suite (Room 606) which comes in at an
eye-watering 5500kr a night. Breakfast
300kr. **1695kr**

THE SQUARE > Rådhuspladsen
14 ☎ 33 38 12 00,
ⓦthesquarecopenhagen.com.
MAP P.33, POCKET MAP A12. Stylish,
smart hotel that is conveniently located
for easy access to Tivoli and the
downtown shopping district. Housed in
a former office block, the minimalist
rooms – spread over five floors – have
been tastefully decorated and come
with all of the required mod cons
discreetly tucked away. The breakfast
restaurant on the sixth floor offers
some great views of the city. Breakfast
178kr. **From 1228kr**

Strøget and the
Inner City

D'ANGLETERRE > Kongens Nytorv 34
☎ 33 12 00 95, ⓦwww.dangleterre
.com. MAP P.40–41, POCKET MAP
E11. Recently reopened after being
refurbished from top to bottom, this
prestigious hotel dating from 1755 is
Copenhagen's answer to *The Ritz* in
London; hotel of choice for anyone
who's anyone, from rock stars to US
presidents. Offering classic elegance,
with modern Danish design kept to
a minimum (although you will find
Bang & Olufsen TV screens above the

Booking ahead

In order to get the lowest room
rate book well in advance or try
one of the many online booking
sites. If you do arrive without a
reservation the city tourist office
should be able to help at their
offices in the airport and on
Vesterbrogade (see p.133) and
online at ⓦvisitcopenhagen.com.

bath tubs), the hotel encompasses a
five-hundred-square-metre luxurious
spa and fitness centre, a grand
restaurant, and a new champagne bar
with over 160 different champagnes
on the menu. Breakfast 570kr. **From
3000kr**

HOTEL SANKT PETRI > Krystalgade
22 ☎ 33 45 91 00, ⓦsktpetri.com.
MAP PP.40–41, POCKET. MAP B11.
Ultra-stylish design hotel housed in
a former five-storey functionalistic
department store. The spacious rooms
have dark parquet flooring and sleek
Scandinavian furniture such as the
super-comfortable Jensen bed. The
hotel is full of business travellers
during the week; you can usually pick
up competitive deals at weekends.
Breakfast 200kr. **1590kr**

Nyhavn and
Frederiksstaden

71 NYHAVN > Nyhavn 71 ☎ 33 43 62
00, ⓦ71nyhavnhotel.com. MAP P.59,
POCKET MAP F11. Two interconnected
converted warehouses overlooking
Inderhavnen and next door to the
city's new playhouse, *71 Nyhavn* is a
charming place to stay. Although it is
slightly on the small side, the hotel's
magnificent location easily makes up
for this slight shortfall. Superior rooms
feature pretty French doors opening
onto a balcony. Primarily a business
hotel, there are some good deals to be
had during summer. Breakfast buffet
170kr. **1419kr**

ADMIRAL HOTEL > Toldbodgade 24 ☎ 33 74 14 14, Ⓦ admiralhotel.dk. MAP P.59, POCKET MAP F11. Romantic waterfront hotel in a vast converted warehouse from 1787 with lots of its original features still intact such as vaulted brick ceilings and enormous wooden beams. There are 300 rooms spread over six floors, each with its own unique charm; a sea view will cost extra. Breakfast is served in the downstairs restaurant *Salt* (p.67) which is also a good bet for other meals, or simply to hang out in its waterfront café section. Breakfast 145kr. **1685kr**

BABETTE GULDSMEDEN > Bredgade 78 ☎ 33 14 15 00, Ⓦ guldsmedenhotels.com. MAP P.59, POCKET MAP G6. Formerly the *Hotel Esplanaden*, the Guldsmeden hotel group have added a touch of luxury to this old building, which overlooks Churchill Parken and Kastellet. There's a rooftop spa and brasserie for real indulgence. Breakfast 175kr. **1295kr**

SØMANDSHJEMMET BETHEL > Nyhavn 22 ☎ 33 13 03 70, Ⓦ hotel-bethel.dk. MAP P.59, POCKET MAP F11. A former hostel for Icelandic sailors, *Bethel*'s superb location overlooking Nyhavn Kanal and the bars and restaurants on the opposite bank can hardly be bettered. Bearing this in mind, the somewhat dated but perfectly comfortable, clean and tidy rooms are excellent value. Ask at reception for a tour of the sailor's church round the back if that's what floats your boat. **845kr**

Rosenborg and around

IBSEN > Vendersgade 23 ☎ 33 13 19 13, Ⓦ arthurhotels.dk/ibsens-hotel. MAP PP.70–71, POCKET MAP A10. Arty hotel situated on a Nansensgade street corner with bright and airy rooms spread over five floors in two interconnected nineteenth-century apartment buildings. Works by local artists (some for sale) are on display throughout the hotel, and the management even supplies art for part payment of rooms (see Ⓦ artmoney.org). Discounted access to Ni'Mat spa next door for 125kr. Breakfast 130kr. **1530kr**

JØRGENSEN > Rømersgade 11 ☎ 33 13 81 86, Ⓦ hoteljoergensen .dk. MAP PP.70–71, POCKET MAP A10. Superb value, slightly run-down hotel-cum-hostel a stone's throw from Torvehallerne. housing a range of rooms in different shapes and sizes, a few with en-suite bathrooms. The tightly packed dorms sleep six to ten and there is no internet access. Breakfast buffet 45kr (included if you book a private room). **Dorm beds 175kr, doubles 750kr**

Christianshavn and Holmen

CPH LIVING > Langebrogade 1C ☎ 61 60 85 46, Ⓦ cphliving.com. MAP P.79, POCKET MAP D14. Absolutely gorgeous hotel boat with twelve identical smartly furnished rooms all facing Christian IV's red-brick brew-house on the opposite bank. Reception is unstaffed and you need an access code to get in, which is given to you when you pay for the room. The reception area doubles as a help-yourself breakfast buffet, which you can eat on the sundeck while taking in the fine views and fresh sea air. Moored next to it is the restaurant boat *Viva* (see p.85). **1460kr**

Vesterbro and Frederiksberg

ABSALON > Helgolandsgade 15 ☎ 33 31 43 44, Ⓦ absalon-hotel .dk. MAP P.87, POCKET MAP D8. Large good-value family-run hotel that has recently been refurbished with en-suite facilities and a fresh, bright decor in the colourful rooms, some of which can accommodate families of up to four. **1100kr**

ANSGAR > Colbjørnsensgade 29 ☎ 33 21 21 96, Ⓦ ansgarhotel.dk. MAP P.87, POCKET MAP A14. Small, friendly recently renovated family hotel in what used to be the dodgy red-light district of Vesterbro. The no-frills tidy

Our top places to stay

For a damn-the-cost weekend: *D'Angleterre* p.121

For romance: *Hotel Central & Café* below

For luxury on a budget: *Hotel Twentyseven* p.120, *Guldsmeden Bertrams* below

For peace and quiet: *Copenhagen Island* below

For Danish design: *Radisson Blu Royal Hotel* p.121

Location, location: *CPH Living* opposite

Watching the pennies: *Løven* below, *Copenhagen Downtown* p.125

rooms are superb value and the price includes a lavish breakfast buffet which in summer is served on an outdoor terrace. **900kr**

CITY HOTEL NEBO > Istedgade 6

☎ 33 21 12 17, Ⓦ nebo.dk. MAP P.87, POCKET MAP D8. Age-old Danish Mission hotel whose profits all go to a Vesterbro homeless shelter behind Central Station. Rooms are nothing to write home about but perfectly pleasant and clean, some with en-suite bathroom, others sharing shower and toilet in the corridor. Breakfast buffet 65kr. **800kr**

COPENHAGEN ISLAND >

Kalvebod Brygge 53 ☎ 33 38 96 00, Ⓦcopenhagenisland.dk. MAP P.87, POCKET MAP D9. The Kim Utzon-designed *Copenhagen Island* is as sleek as it gets. With wonderful large windows looking out to the Copencabana harbour pool just outside, you could be excused for thinking that you're on a seaside holiday. Inside the stylish rooms are beautifully furnished with modern Danish design and top of the range electronics. In the hotel basement there's a fitness centre with steam bath and sauna. Breakfast 150kr. **1195kr**

GULDSMEDEN AXEL >

Helgolandsgade 8 ☎ 33 31 32 66, Ⓦ hotelguldsmeden.dk/axel. MAP P.87, POCKET MAP D8. Among the city's most appealing boutique hotels with beautiful Balinese-inspired decor and superb attention to detail. This is where the supermodels come to stay and you're likely to feel like one of them after a couple of days, your every whim being catered for by the super-attentive staff. Given the level of pampering, all

this comes at a very reasonable price. Breakfast buffet 175kr. **1490kr**

GULDSMEDEN BERTRAMS >

Vesterbrogade 107 ☎ 70 20 81 07, Ⓦ hotelguldsmeden.dk/bertrams. MAP P.87, POCKET MAP C8. Another of the Guldsmeden (Dragonfly) boutique hotel chain (see above), this one styling French colonial decor with wonderful dark wooden furniture and the occasional fake fur laying around. Not as large as the *Axel* branch, *Bertrams* has a slightly more personable and intimate feel, not least as the intimidating fashion-week types don't tend to stay here. Breakfast 140kr. No under-18s. **1490kr**

HOTEL CENTRAL & CAFÉ >

Tullinsgade 1 ☎ 33 21 00 95, Ⓦ centralhotelogcafe.dk. MAP P.87, POCKET MAP C8. Set above an appropriately tiny (five-seat) coffeeshop and once inhabited by a cobbler, this one-room spot definitely earns its billing as "the smallest hotel in the world". A bed, bathroom and flat-screen TV are squeezed into the twelve-metre-square room that nevertheless beckons with some real attention to detail and olde-worlde charm. **1800kr**

LØVEN > Vesterbrogade 30 ☎ 33 79

67 20, Ⓦ loevenhotel.dk. MAP P.87, POCKET MAP D8. A basic hotel on noisy Vesterbrogade, the real benefit of *Løven* is its excellent value and the lively and very helpful owner who runs it as a tight ship. The plain rooms come with up to five beds, some sharing facilities, others en suite. Though there's no breakfast on offer, there's a fully fitted kitchen should you wish to self-cater. Wi-fi is only available in the kitchen. **590kr**

SAGA HOTEL > Colbjørnsensgade 18-20 ☎ 33 24 49 44, ⓦ sagahotel .dk. MAP P.87, POCKET MAP D8. In the once grotty red-light district of Vesterbro, family-run *Saga* is today one of the city's really good budget options and popular with backpackers who've had their fill of rowdy and impersonal hostels. The sparsely decorated rooms sleeping up to five mostly share facilities although there are also a few en-suite rooms. Filling breakfasts are served on the second floor in a cosy dining area. **950kr**

SCT THOMAS > Frederiksberg Allé 7 ☎ 33 21 64 64, ⓦ hotelsctthomas .dk. MAP P.87, POCKET MAP C8. Popular small Frederiksberg hotel housed in a nineteenth-century apartment block not far from lively Værnedamsvej and offering simple uncluttered rooms. The buffet breakfast, served in the newly excavated basement, is one of the best in town. Free internet only in the lobby. **795kr**

WAKE UP COPENHAGEN > Carsten Niebuhrs Gade 11 ☎ 44 80 00 00, ⓦ wakeupcopenhagen.com. MAP P.87, POCKET MAP D9. Super-efficient and slightly impersonal, this brand-new budget hotel on the edge of Vesterbro overlooks the railway line to one side and Inner Havnen to the other. Spread over nine floors, the 500-odd a/c rooms verge on the small side but feel perfectly adequate thanks to the clever design and layout created by architect Kim Utzon. Larger rooms and rooms with a better view cost more. Breakfast 70kr. **850kr**

ZLEEP HOTEL CENTRUM > Helgolandsgade 14 ☎ 70 23 56 35, ⓦ zleephotels.com. MAP P.87, POCKET MAP D8. No-frills accommodation a stone's throw from Central Station, this really is as Spartan as it gets. Hence the very reasonable prices, particularly if you book far in advance. Part of a wider Zleep concept chain, the hotel provides largely self-service accommodation with food and drink available from vending machines – although the basic breakfast buffet (89kr) is manned. Rooms sleep up to four. **499kr**

Nørrebro and Østerbro

AVENUE > Åboulevard 29 ☎ 35 37 31 11, ⓦ avenuehotel.dk. MAP P.97, POCKET MAP C6. Out from the centre on the border between Nørrebro and Frederiksberg, *Avenue* has three key things going for it: the spacious classically furnished rooms, free parking, and very reasonable rates. It also has the added bonus of not being part of a chain, which gives it that personable vibe that makes you feel right at home. **1020kr**

HOTEL RYE > Ryesgade 115 ☎ 35 26 52 10, ⓦ hotelrye.dk. MAP P.98, POCKET MAP E4. Homely *Hotel Rye* is a brilliant option away from the city centre yet near the lively lake area of Østerbro and the tranquil Fælledparken. Housed in a former care home, the sixteen highly individualized rooms are spread over the second and third floors of an apartment building. All have shared bathroom in the hall (you are provided with a kimono and slippers for nocturnal visits). Outside the back yard is equipped with a play area for kids, and in the cosy dining area freshly baked rolls are available with breakfast every morning. **900kr**

Hostels

Copenhagen has some excellent hostels that can often rival budget hotels in terms of value and style. Many offer private doubles, twins and triples as well as the usual dorm rooms. Be aware that the latter are often packed with rowdy Swedish students during the summer holidays and availability can be an issue at these times. Danhostel (w danhostel.dk) which runs two of the hostels below charges a one-off membership fee of 70kr if you don't hold a Hostelling International card. Note that *Jørgensen* (see p.122) also offers dorm beds.

COPENHAGEN DOWNTOWN > Vandkunsten 5 ☎ 70 23 21 10, w copenhagendowntown.com. MAP PP.40–41, POCKET MAP C12. Though affiliated to Danhostel, *Copenhagen Downtown* has a hip, independent feel with guests sprawling on bean bags out onto the pavement, and a cool retro Scandinavian design. The location right next to some superb music venues and a plethora of watering holes is also hard to beat. Rooms are on the smallish side sleeping two to ten people in bunk beds, usually with shared bathroom, but everything is clean and tidy and the vibe energetic. Breakfast 65kr. **Dorm beds 210kr, doubles 660kr**

DANHOSTEL CITY > H.C Andersens Boulevard 50 ☎ 33 11 85 85, w danhostelcopenhagencity.dk. MAP P.33, POCKET MAP C14. Modern five-star hostel housed in Denmark's first high-rise building, dating from 1955. Encompassing over a thousand beds in four-, six-, eight- and ten-bed rooms spread over sixteen floors it offers wonderful views over Copenhagen. Add the interior design by GUBI and facilities such as a bar-café in the lobby and games room in the basement and you could be forgiven for thinking that you're staying at a modern hotel albeit one with bunk beds. Breakfast 75kr. **Dorm beds 195kr, doubles 615kr**

GENERATOR > Adelgade 5–7 ☎ 78 77 54 00, w generatorhostels .com. MAP PP.70–71, POCKET MAP D10. Part of a Europe-wide chain of funky hostels, this one is housed in an apartment block designed by Phillipe Starck. It's one of the best places to stay in town if you're young and adventurous, but like your creature comforts. All rooms come with en-suite bathrooms and range from twin-bed doubles to (pink) female dorms sleeping six and mixed dorms sleeping eight. The hostel also offers plenty of places to chill out including a large outdoor terrace and a spacious lounge/bar boasting an enormous TV. Breakfast 75kr. **Dorm beds 250kr, doubles 720k**

URBAN HOUSE > Colbjørnsensgade 5–11 ☎ 33 23 29 29, w urbanhouse .me. MAP P.87, POCKET MAP D8. This trendy hostel/hotel opened in 2015 with 950 beds in 225 rooms. Dorms and private rooms (sleep 1–4 people), plus an in-house bike shop and tattoo studio. Breakfast 75kr. **Dorms from 175kr, doubles from 750kr**

Arrival

However you arrive in Copenhagen you'll find yourself within easy reach of the city centre. Copenhagen Airport is just a few kilometres to the southeast, on the edge of the island of Amager, while almost all trains and buses deposit you near the city's main transport hub, Central Station.

By air

Getting into the city from **Copenhagen Airport** (wcph.dk), 11km from the city in the suburb of Kastrup, couldn't be easier: one of Europe's fastest airport-to-city rail lines runs directly to Central Station (roughly every 10min; 14min; 36kr). In addition, the metro (every 4–6min during the day, every 15–20min midnight–7am) links the airport with Christianshavn (12min), Kongens Nytorv (13min) and Nørreport (15min) stations (all 36kr) in the centre. Copenhagen Airport is in Zone 3 (see opposite). A taxi to the centre costs about 250–300kr – there's a rank outside the arrivals hall.

You can pick up free maps from the helpful information desk in sleek Terminal 3 (daily 6.10am–11pm). They also sell Copenhagen Cards (see box opposite). The airport has two late-opening banks (daily 6am–10pm), lots of ATMs, free wi-fi throughout, 72-hour luggage storage lockers (see p.132), numerous car rental agencies and a post office. The stylish *Hilton Hotel*, connected to the airport by a pedestrian walkway, is a good place to kill some time – their lobby bar is equipped with arrival and departure screens.

Buses from small **Malmö Airport** in Sweden (wswedavia.com/malmo; see box, p.114) are integrated with flight arrivals. Some 60km east of Copenhagen, it has retained its role as a hub for budget flights to the city. The one-hour bus journey with Gråhundsbus (wgraahundbus.dk; 100kr) skirts around Malmö itself before crossing the magnificent Öresund Bridge (p.115), reason enough in itself to opt for the cheaper airfare option.

By bus and train

All buses and trains to Copenhagen arrive at or near **Central Station** (in Danish, Hovedbanegården or København H), the city's main transport hub, from where there are excellent connections to virtually every part of the city via bus or local train – and as from 2019 also a new metro circular line (see opposite). The station also has an array of shops, a foreign-exchange bureau (daily 8am–9pm), places to eat and, downstairs, left-luggage lockers (see p.132). The national train company, DSB, has a travel agency and information centre just inside the main entrance off Vesterbrogade (Mon–Fri 7am–8pm, Sat 8am–4pm, Sun 8am–5pm; ☎70 13 14 15, wdsb.dk) and an easy-to-use ticket machine in the hallway (daily 4.30am–2.40am).

Eurolines coaches from around Europe stop behind the station on Ingerslevgade, across from DGI-byen. Buses from Malmö airport stop in front of *Plaza Hotel* next to the station.

Getting around

The best way to explore Copenhagen is either to walk or cycle: the inner city is compact, much of the central area pedestrianized, and there's a comprehensive network of excellent bike paths. For travelling further afield, there's an integrated network of buses, metros, S-Tog (urban rapid

The Copenhagen Card

If you plan to do lots of sightseeing, you might want to buy a **Copenhagen Card**. Valid for 24, 42, 72 or 120 hours (359kr/499kr/589kr/799kr), it covers public transport (including Helsingør and Roskilde) and gives free (or discounted) entry to most museums. This can save a lot of money – especially since it can also give you twenty- to fifty-percent off car rental, ferry rides and theatre tickets. You can either book the card in advance online at ⓦwww.copenhagencard.com or pick one up on arrival at the airport, visitor centre or Central Station.

transit) and local trains.

Tickets

All city transport operates on a **zonal system** encompassing the metro, trains and buses. The city centre and immediate area, as you'd expect, are in zones 1 and 2. The cheapest ticket (**billet**) costs 24kr and is valid for one hour's travel within any two zones, with unlimited transfers between buses and trains. There's an excellent-value **24-hour ticket** (130kr), which is valid on all transport to as far away as Helsingør and Roskilde, as well as night buses. Finally, if you're planning on visiting lots of museums and attractions, the Copenhagen Card (see box above) also includes free transport.

Tickets can be bought on board buses or at train stations, while 24-hour tickets are only available at bus or train stations and HT Kortsalg kiosks. Route maps can be picked up free at stations, and most free city maps include bus lines and a diagram of the S-Tog and metro network. For more information see ⓦmoviatrafik.dk/dinrejse/tourist.

The metro

Copenhagen's fast and efficient underground **metro system** (ⓦm.dk) circumvents the Central Station in a "U" shape, connecting the island of Amager and Copenhagen airport with west Copenhagen via

Christianshavn and Kongens Nytorv. The metro's two lines – M1 and M2 – cross the S-Tog and regional trains at Nørreport, Flintholm and Vanløse. A new circular line, due to open in 2019, will integrate more effectively with the S-Tog system stopping also at Hovedbanegården and Østerport. Metro stations are marked by a large red underlined "M" painted onto aluminium pillars.

S-Tog and regular trains

The **S-Tog** rapid transit service (ⓦs-tog.dk) is laid out in a huge "U" shape and covers the whole Copenhagen metropolitan area. Six of its seven lines stop at Central Station, with the others circling the centre. Each line has a letter and is also colour-coded on route maps. Stations are marked by red hexagonal signs with a yellow "S" inside them.

Regular national trains are run by the **Danish State Railway** (DSB; ⓦdsb.dk) and among other towns connect the city to Helsingør and Roskilde, calling at Østerport and Nørreport stations and some suburban destinations on the way.

Buses

The city's **bus** network (ⓦmoviatrafik .dk) is more comprehensive than the S-Tog system and can be a more convenient way to get around once you get the hang of finding the stops – marked by yellow placards on signposts – and as long as you avoid the rush hour (7–9am & 5–6pm). The vast majority stop at Rådhuspladsen next to Tivoli. Buses with an "S" suffix only make limited stops, offering a faster service – check they make the stop you require before you get on. Buses with an "A" suffix indicate that the bus runs frequently. All buses have a small electronic board above the driver's seat displaying both the zone you're currently in and the time – so there's no excuse for not having a valid ticket. A skeletal **night-bus** (*natdrift*) runs once or twice an hour (fares remain the same). Night-bus numbers always end with "N".

Harbour buses

A cheaper way to experience Copenhagen from the waterfront than a canal tour (see box opposite), yellow **harbour "buses"** sail along the harbour between Nordre Toldbod (near the Little Mermaid) and the Royal Library, stopping six times and costing the same as a normal bus fare. Services (daily every 20min about 7am–7pm) are cancelled when the harbour is frozen.

Cycling

If the weather's good, the best way to see Copenhagen is to do as the locals do and get on your bike. The superb, city-wide cycle lanes make **cycling** very safe and bikes can be taken on S-Tog trains (free of charge) through any number of zones. Lights are mandatory at night (you'll be stopped and fined if the police catch you without them). Despite a recent campaign to promote wearing helmets few locals do so. You can usually **rent bikes** through your hotel or hostel (around 100kr/day). Otherwise try Københavns Cyklebørs, Gothersgade

157, Indre By (Mon–Fri 9am–5.30pm, Sat 10am–1.30pm; ☎33 14 07 17, ⓦcykelboersen.dk; 75kr/day, 350kr/week, 300kr deposit); Pedal Atleten, Oslo Plads 9, next to Østerport Station (Mon–Fri 8am–6pm, Sat 10am–3pm; ☎33 33 85 13, ⓦpedalatleten.dk; 100kr/day, 375kr/week, 500kr deposit); or Baisikeli, Turesensgade 10, Indre By and Ingerslevsgade 80 (daily 9am–4/6pm; ☎26 70 02 29, ⓦbaisikeli.dk; from 50kr for six hours, 270kr/week, 200kr deposit).

Taxis

Taxis are plentiful, but with a flat starting fare of 24kr, then 15kr per kilometre (19kr after 4pm and at weekends), they're only worth taking in a group. There's a handy rank outside Central Station; you can also book with Taxa (☎35 35 35 35) or hail one in the street – the green "Fri" sign on top shows it's available. Rickshaw-styled **cycle taxis** (April–Oct; ☎35 43 01 22, ⓦrickshaw.dk), carrying a maximum of two people, operate a flat starting fare of 40kr if you flag them down on the street, then charge 4kr per minute.

Directory A–Z

Addresses

The street name is always written before the house number, which is followed by the apartment number or floor the apartment is on, followed by the side the apartment is at (t.h. – to the right as you come up the stairs, and t.v. – to the left). So, Læssøesgade 16 3 t.h., means the third-floor apartment to the right, in building number 16 on Læssøesgade. The city is divided into postal districts consisting of four digits followed by the area so Indre

Guided Tours

As well as the operators below, the Copenhagen Visitor Centre on Vesterbrogade (see p.133) has a long list of English-language guided walking tours many of which are free.

Bike Copenhagen with Mike ☎26 39 56 88, ⓦbikecopenhagenwithmike.dk. Cycle tours to Vesterbro, Amalienborg, the Little Mermaid, Christiania and much more, led by the knowledgeable and charismatic Mike. No booking required. 299kr including bike. Cash only.

Copenhagen Sightseeing Tours ⓦsightseeing.dk. A variety of bus tours (including hop-on hop-off routes which cover stretches by canal boat) with multilingual headphone commentary. From 175kr.

Copenhagen Food Tours ☎50 12 36 45, ⓦcopenhagen.foodtours.eu. Two-hour (Mon–Fri 2.30pm, 400kr) and four-hour (Mon–Sat 10am; 700kr) walking tours sampling tasters from the latest movers and shakers on the Danish food scene. The tasters along the way add up to a full-blown meal, so best to arrive hungry. Tours start and end at Torvehallerne.

Kajak Ole ☎40 50 40 06, ⓦkajakole.dk. Kayak tours (April–Oct) giving a unique view of the city from the water. Choose between a 90min paddle around Christianshavn to a 3hr circumnavigation of Slotsholmen. From 295kr including a canalside drink. Tours start from in front of *Færge Caféen*.

Netto-Bådene ☎32 54 41 02, ⓦhavnerundfart.dk. Excellent-value one-hour canal tours departing from Holmens Kirke and taking in Nyhavn, Holmen, Nyholm, Amalienborg Palace and the Little Mermaid. 40kr.

By is Kbh K preceded by a four-digit number; Østerbro is Kbh Ø, Nørrebro Kbh N, Vesterbro Kbh V, Amager Kbh S and Frederiksberg Fred. After the completion of the bridge across to Sweden the city of Malmö is jokingly called Kbh M.

Cinema

International blockbusters are screened at Imperial (Ved Vesterport 4 ☎70 13 12 11, ⓦnfbio.dk/imperial). More alternative films are shown at Grand Teatret (Mikkel Bryggersgade 8 ☎33 15 16 11, ⓦgrandteatret.dk) and Vester Vov Vov (Absalonsgade 5 ☎33 24 42 00, ⓦvestervovvov.dk).

Crime

Copenhagen has an extremely low crime rate. Keep an eye on your cash and passport and you should have little reason to visit the **police**. If you do, you'll find them courteous and usually able to speak English. The central police station is at Politorvet 14 (☎33 14 88 88).

Electricity

The Danish electricity supply runs at 220–240V, 50Hz AC; sockets generally require a two-pin plug. Visitors from the UK will need an adaptor; visitors from outside the EU may need a transformer.

Embassies and consulates

Australia Dampfærgevej 26, 2nd floor ☎70 26 36 76; Canada Kristen Bernikowsgade 1 ☎33 48 32 00; Ireland Østbanegade 21 ☎35 47 32 00; South Africa Gammel Vartov 8, Hellerup ☎39 18 01 55; UK Kastelsvej 36–40 ☎35 44 52 00; US Dag Hammerskjölds Allé 24 ☎33 41 71 00.

Emergency numbers

Dial ☎112 for police, fire or ambulance.

Gay and lesbian Copenhagen

Copenhagen is one of the world's top gay destinations. Attitudes are very tolerant and there is a lively gay scene enjoyed by many straight people, too. The Copenhagen Pride festival (see p.134) is a particularly great time to experience gay Copenhagen. Check out ⌨www .copenhagen-gay-life.dk for what's on.

Health

There are **24-hour emergency departments** at Bispebjerg Hospital, Bispebjerg Bakke 23 (☎35 31 35 31) and Hvidovre Hospital, Kettegårds Alle 30 (☎36 32 36 32). If you need a **doctor**, call ☎70 13 00 41 (after 4pm or on weekends). For **dental emergencies**, contact Tandlægevagten, Oslo Plads 14 ☎1813 (Mon–Fri 8am–9.30pm, Sat & Sun 10am–noon).

The city's two main 24-hour **pharmacies** are Steno Apotek, Vesterbrogade 6C in front of Central Station (☎33 14 82 66) and Sønderbro Apotek, Amagerbrogade 158, Amager (☎32 58 01 40).

Internet

Copenhagen has plenty of wireless hubs in cafés and bars and on trains. Most hotels and hostels – and even some campsites – offer wi-fi (most for free), and access is also available **free** at libraries (though not the Royal Library).

Left luggage

The DSB Garderobe office downstairs in Central Station **stores luggage** for 55/65kr per item per day and has lockers (Mon–Sat 5.30am–1am, Sun 6am–1am; 50kr/60kr for 24hr). Copenhagen airport's left-luggage facility, in Parking House P4 across the road from terminal 2 (open 24hr), has small and large lockers for 50kr and 75kr per day respectively (max 3 days).

Lost property

The police department's **lost-property** office is at Slotsherrensvej 113, Vanløse ☎38 74 88 22. For items lost on a bus, contact the bus information office on ☎36 13 14 15 (Mon–Fri 9am–2pm); for items lost on a train or S-Tog, there's a lost luggage office at Central Station (Mon–Fri 8am–8pm, Sat & Sun 10am–5pm) or contact them on ☎24 68 09 60 (Mon–Fri 10am–1pm); for lost property at Copenhagen Airport go to Terminal 3 or look online at ⌨missingx.com.

Money

The Danish currency is the **krone** (plural kroner), made up of 100 øre, and comes in notes of 1000kr, 500kr, 200kr, 100kr and 50kr, and coins of 20kr, 10kr, 5kr, 2kr, 1kr, 50øre. At the time of writing, the exchange rate was approximately 10.10kr to the pound, 7.45kr to the euro and 6.70kr to the US dollar. For the latest rates, go to ⌨xe.com.

PIN codes are always required when paying by card. If your card is lost or stolen, PBS Net (24hr ☎44 89 27 50) can block your card.

Opening hours

Shops tend to open Mon–Thurs 10am–6pm, Fri 10am–7pm, Sat 10am–4pm, Sun noon–4pm but shops in the centre of town tend to have longer hours. Most offices are open Mon–Fri 9am–4/4.30pm.

Phones

You should be able to use your **mobile phone** though it may be cheaper to

Public holidays

Denmark observes most religious holidays and moveable feasts. On the following days, expect all banks and most shops to be closed, and check the websites of attractions. Easter is a five-day holiday, followed by a number of single religious holidays up until Whitsuntide.

December 31 New Year; **January 1** New Year's Day; Maundy Thursday; Good Friday; Easter Sunday; Easter Monday; *Store Bededay* (Day of Repentance and Prayer, 4th Friday after Easter); Ascension Day (6th Thurs after Easter); Whitsun (Sun & Mon, 7 weeks after Easter); **December 24** Christmas Eve; **December 25** Christmas Day; **December 26** Boxing Day.

buy a Danish SIM card. For 99kr, you'll get a Danish number plus about forty minutes of domestic calls. The most commonly used network is TDC, but coverage with Telemore, Telenor and others is just as good. SIM cards and credit can be bought in supermarkets, kiosks and phone shops.

Calling Denmark from abroad, the **international code** is ☏45. For **collect international calls** from Denmark dial ☏80 30 40 00 – instructions for this "Country Direct" system are in phone booths (in English), call ☏80 60 40 50 for free assistance.

Post
It can be hard to find a post office these days, although there is still one inside Central Station (Mon–Fri 9am–7pm, Sat noon–4pm). Mail under 50g costs 25kr (within Europe) or 30kr (rest of the world). You can buy stamps from most newsagents.

Smoking
Smoking is banned in all public buildings and restaurants as well as on station concourses and platforms. Bars and cafés under forty square metres which do not serve fresh food may still allow smoking.

Time
Denmark is one hour ahead of GMT, six hours ahead of US Eastern Standard Time, and nine ahead of US Pacific Standard Time.

Tipping
Service is included on all restaurant, hotel and taxi bills, so unless you feel you've been given exceptionally good service, tipping is not necessary.

Tourist information
The Copenhagen Visitor Centre (Mon–Fri 9am–4pm, Sat 9am–2pm; ☏70 22 24 42, ⓦvisitcopenhagen .com), across the road from the Central Station at Vesterbrogade 4A, offers maps, general information and accommodation reservations, along with free accommodation-booking terminals.

Travellers with disabilities
Copenhagen is a model city for travellers with disabilities: wheelchair access, facilities and help are generally available at hotels, hostels, museums and public places. To see whether a place caters for travellers with disabilities, check the website ⓦgodadgang.dk or contact the tourist office at ⓦvisitcopenhagen.com.

Travelling with children
Copenhagen is a very child-friendly city with reserved children's pram areas on buses and trains, and children's menus and high seats available at most restaurants. The low level of traffic and many pedestrianized streets also make for a stress-free visit with kids. For more ideas, see p.10.

Festivals and events

CPH:PIX

Eighteen-day film festival in April
ⓦcphpix.dk
The city's premier film festival which features a wide range of Danish as well as classic international films in their original language. Most of the city's cinemas take part.

COPENHAGEN BEER FESTIVAL

Long weekend in May ⓦale.dk
A new and already very popular festival housed in the recently reopened TAP1 bottling hall in the Carlsberg area, featuring over a thousand different beers from around the world.

COPENHAGEN CARNIVAL

Whitsun weekend ⓦkarneval-kbh.dk
A mini Rio of samba and colourful costumes along Strøget and Købmagergade which culminates in all-night partying at Fælledparken supposedly allowing you to see the Whitsun sun "dance" as it rises in the early hours of the morning.

SANKT HANS AFTEN

Midsummer's eve ⓦvisitcopenhagen.com
Bonfires and traditional Danish folksongs at various locations along the Copenhagen coast. Check the tourist board website for locations and times.

ROSKILDE FESTIVAL

Last week of June or first week of July
(see box p.111) ⓦroskilde-festival.dk
Four-day Glastonbury-style music festival in the outskirts of Roskilde preceded by four days' warm-up in the camping area.

COPENHAGEN JAZZ FESTIVAL

First or second week of July ⓦjazz.dk
Local and international jazz stars – young and old – take over the city's music stages and venues, as well as many outside spaces, making it Europe's biggest jazz event. With loads of free gigs the entire city seems to be swinging to all sorts of jazz imaginable.

COPENHAGEN PRIDE

One week in July or August ⓦcopenhagenpride.dk
Superb week of gay events focused on the area around Frederiksholms Kanal and culminating in the flamboyant and colourful Gay Pride Parade which makes its way through the centre of town on the festival Saturday.

COPENHAGEN COOKING

Last ten days of August ⓦcopenhagencooking.dk
Riding on the Nordic cuisine popularity wave, over one hundred events across the city hosted by many of the city's famous chefs give you an opportunity to sample some of the amazing creations.

CHRISTMAS AND NEW YEARS

Leading up to Christmas – which is celebrated Christmas Eve – the city is aglow with festive lights and decorations, and *gløgg* and *æbleskiver* (a version of mulled wine and dough balls with apple inside) is sold everywhere. On New Year's Eve Rådhuspladsen is the scene of a massive fireworks fest, champagne drinking and kissing of strangers.

Chronology

1043 > The name "Havn" appears in the Knýtlinga Saga, described as the place Norwegian king Magnus sought cover after being defeated at sea.

1160 > Bishop Absalon is given control over "Havn" by his foster brother King Valdemar. Recent excavations have shown that Copenhagen at the time was a significant fishing village – Kongens Nytorv largely built on fish bones – and its residents unusually tall.

1167 > Bishop Absalon completes the construction of fortified Københavns Slot on present day's Slotholmen Island. Its aim is to protect the town's fishermen and traders from Wendish pirates.

1238 > The construction of the town's first monastery commences – today's Helligåndshus.

1249 > The earliest recorded attack and plunder of the town by a Hanseatic fleet from Lübeck.

1334 > With 5000 inhabitants Copenhagen is Scandinavia's largest settlement.

1369 > The town is attacked and briefly occupied by Hanseatic forces who systematically dismantle Københavns Slot.

1417 > King Eric of Pomerania makes the newly reconstructed Københavns Slot his seat of power and residence of the royal family.

1443 > Copenhagen replaces Roskilde as Denmark's capital.

1479 > Copenhagen University, the first in Scandinavia, is established in today's Latin Quarter.

1536 > Protestant Reformation takes hold with the arrest of the Catholic Bishop of Copenhagen.

1588 > Christian IV aka "The Builder King" is born. After taking the throne at the age of ten he begins a lifelong programme of works. Among his many feats are the neighbourhood of Christianshavn, the city's defensive ring of moats, ramparts and Kastellet, Rosenborg Slot and Rundetårn.

1657 > Skåne is ceded to Sweden at the Treaty of Roskilde, Denmark's second most important town Malmö thereby becoming Swedish.

1659 > After three years' siege, the city is stormed by Swedish troops.

1660 > Absolute monarchy is introduced.

1711 > Plague epidemic kills at least 22,000.

1728 > The first "great fire" of Copenhagen destroys over a thousand buildings

1730 > Christian VI decides to have Københavns Slot torn down and a much grander Louis XIV Rococo-style palace – renamed Christiansborg – is erected in its stead. It burns to the ground 28 years after its completion in 1766. Only the stables and riding ground survive.

1795 > The second great fire of Copenhagen burns Christiansborg to the ground.

1801 > British and Danish ships engage at the Battle of Copenhagen. Horatio Nelson famously turns a blind eye to Admiral Sir Hyde Parker's orders to retreat.

1807 > Fearing the Danes may side with Napoleon, the Royal Navy shells Copenhagen. After three nights of bombardment, large parts of the city lie in ruins. The Danish-Norwegian navy is surrendered to the British.

1828 > A new Romanesque-style Christiansborg is completed.

1836 > Hans Christian Andersen's *The Little Mermaid* is published.

1838 > Sculptor Bertel Thorvaldsen returns to Copenhagen after forty years in Rome.

1843 > George Carstensen's brainchild Tivoli opens in the former rampart area.

1843 > Father of Existentialism Søren Kierkegaard's *Either/Or* is published.

1847 > J.C. Jacobsen founds the Carlsberg brewery.

1884 > The second Christiansborg is burnt to the ground leaving only Christiansborgs Slotskirke standing.

1897 > The Ny Carlsberg Glyptotek is opened by philanthropic brewing magnate Carl Jacobsen, son of J.C.

1911 > The National Romantic Central Station stands completed.

1913 > The Little Mermaid statue by Edvard Eriksen (and paid for by Carl Jacobsen) is unveiled.

1928 > The current neo-Baroque Christiansborg is completed.

1940 > In the early hours of April 9, Copenhagen is occupied by German forces with barely a shot fired.

1943–1945 > Most of Denmark's Jewish population is smuggled successfully across to Sweden in fishing boats.

1971 > First Roskilde festival.

1971 > Christiania is founded in disused military barracks on Christianshavn.

1972 > Queen Margrethe II ascends the throne.

1973 > Denmark joins the EU.

1992 > The Danish football team beat Germany to win the European Cup, receiving a heroes' welcome on their return home.

2000 > The Øresunds link to Sweden is opened.

2005 > Crown Prince Frederik marries his Tasmanian bride Mary.

2007 > Copenhagen-based crime drama *The Killing* becomes an international hit (along with its woolly jumpers).

2010 > Copenhagen's *Noma* is rated as the world's best restaurant.

2011 > Work begins on a new city circle metro line, due to open in 2019; construction unearths some remarkable archeological finds.

2012 > Copenhagen's first official bicycle super highway opens.

2014 > Copenhagen hosts the Eurovision Song Contest in a former shipyard on Papirøen, spending three times its budget.

Danish

In general, English is widely understood throughout Denmark, as is German, and young people especially often speak both fluently. However, even with little need to resort to Danish, learning a few phrases will surprise and delight any Danes you meet. If you can speak Swedish or Norwegian, then you should have little problem making yourself understood – all three languages share the same root.

There is no single word in the Danish language for "please". So when a Dane doesn't say "please" when speaking to you in English, it's not because they're rude – the word just doesn't come naturally. Danes are also renowned for being direct – if they want something they say "Give me..." – which can, incorrectly, be interpreted as impolite.

An idea of pronunciation for key phrases is given in brackets below.

Basic words and phrases

Taler de engelsk? (tayla dee ENgellsg)	Do you speak English?
Ja (ya)	Yes
Nej (nye)	No
Jeg forstår det ikke (yai fus TO day igge)	I don't understand
Værså venlig (verso venli)	Please (or the nearest thing to)
Tak (tagg)	Thank you
Undskyld (unsgul)	Excuse me
Hi (hye)	Hello/Hi
Godmorgen (goMORN)	Good morning
Goddag (goDA)	Good afternoon
Godnat (goNAD)	Goodnight
Farvel (faVELL)	Goodbye
Hvor er? (voa ea?)	Where is?
Hvad koster det? (vath kosta day?)	How much does it cost?

Jeg vil gerne ha... (yai vay GERna ha)	I'd like...
Hvor er toiletterne? (voa ea toaLETTaneh?)	Where are the toilets?
Et bord til ... (et boa te...)	A table for...
Må jeg bede om regningen? (moah yai beyde uhm RYningan?)	Can I have the bill/check, please?
Billet (billed)	Ticket

Food and drink basics

Bøfsandwich	Hamburger
Brød	Bread
Det kolde bord	Help-yourself cold buffet
Is	Ice cream
Ostebord	Cheese board
Peber	Pepper
Pølser	Frankfurters/sausages
Rugbrød	Rye bread
Salt	Salt
Sildebord	A selection of spiced and pickled herring
Kylling	Chicken
Oksekød	Beef
Svinekød	Pork
Kartofler	Potatoes
Fisk	Fish
Smør	Butter
Smørrebrød	Open sandwiches
Sukker	Sugar
Wienerbrød	"Danish" pastry
Øl	Beer
Fadøl	Draught beer
Guldøl	Strong beer
Vin	Wine
Husets vin	House wine
Hvidvin	White wine
Rødvin	Red wine
Mineralvand	Mineral water
Chokolade (varm)	Chocolate (hot)
Kærnemælk	Buttermilk
Kaffe (med fløde)	Coffee (with cream)
Mælk	Milk
Te	Tea
Vand	Water

PUBLISHING INFORMATION

This second edition published April 2016 by **Rough Guides Ltd**

80 Strand, London WC2R 0RL

11, Community Centre, Panchsheel Park, New Delhi 110017, India

Distributed by Penguin Random House

Penguin Books Ltd, 80 Strand, London WC2R 0RL

Penguin Group (USA) 345 Hudson Street, NY 10014, USA

Penguin Group (Australia) 250 Camberwell Road, Camberwell, Victoria 3124, Australia

Penguin Group (NZ) 67 Apollo Drive, Mairangi Bay, Auckland 1310, New Zealand

Penguin Group (South Africa) Block D, Rosebank Office Park, 181 Jan Smuts Avenue, Parktown North, Gauteng, South Africa 2193

Rough Guides is represented in Canada by

Tourmaline Editions Inc., 662 King Street West, Suite 304, Toronto, Ontario, M5V 1M7

Typeset in Minion and Din to an original design by Henry Iles and Dan May.

Printed and bound in China

© Rough Guides 2016

Maps © Rough Guides. Copenhagen Transport map reproduced with permission of DOT/Damsgaard & Lange, 2015.

144pp includes index

A catalogue record for this book is available from the British Library

ISBN 978-0-24123-853-0

The publishers and authors have done their best to ensure the accuracy and currency of all the information in **Pocket Rough Guide Copenhagen**, however, they can accept no responsibility for any loss, injury, or inconvenience sustained by any traveller as a result of information or advice contained in the guide.

1 3 5 7 9 8 6 4 2

ROUGH GUIDES CREDITS

Editor: Olivia Rawes

Layout: Pradeep Thapliyal

Cartography: Ed Wright

Picture editor: Michelle Bhatia

Photographer: Diana Jarvis

Proofreader: Karen Parker

Managing editor: Monica Woods

Production: Jimmy Lao

Cover photo research: Sarah Stewart-Richardson

Editorial assistant: Freya Godfrey

Senior pre-press designer: Dan May

Publisher: Keith Drew

Publishing director: Georgina Dee

HELP US UPDATE

We've gone to a lot of effort to ensure that the second edition of **Pocket Rough Guide Copenhagen** is accurate and up-to-date. However, things change – places get "discovered", opening hours are notoriously fickle, restaurants and rooms raise prices or lower standards. If you feel we've got it wrong or left something out, we'd like to know, and if you can remember the address, the price, the hours, the phone number, so much the better.

Please send your comments with the subject line "**Pocket Rough Guide Copenhagen Update**" to mail@roughguides.com. We'll credit all contributions and send a copy of the next edition (or any other Rough Guide if you prefer) for the very best emails.

Find travel information, connect with fellow travellers and book your trip on ⓦ roughguides.com

THE UPDATER

Jane Graham was born in Yorkshire with no ties to Scandinavia other than a Viking-like sense of adventure. She moved to Copenhagen in 1999 and stayed, keeping busy as writer, editor, translator and mum to four.

PHOTO CREDITS

Index

Maps are marked in **bold**.

SO NOW WE'VE TOLD YOU
ABOUT THE THINGS NOT TO
MISS, THE BEST PLACES TO
STAY, THE TOP RESTAURANTS,
THE LIVELIEST BARS AND THE
MOST SPECTACULAR SIGHTS,
IT ONLY SEEMS FAIR TO
TELL YOU ABOUT THE BEST
TRAVEL INSURANCE AROUND